Saint Louise de Marillac
Servant of the Poor

A painting of St. Louise. She urged the Daughters of Charity to treat the poor with great gentleness, respect, and courtesy, for "The poor are the members of Jesus Christ."

Saint Louise de Marillac
Servant of the Poor

by
Sister Vincent Regnault, D.C.

Translated from the French by
Sister Louise Sullivan, D.C.

"Amen I say to you, as long as you did it to one of these my least brethren, you did it to me."
—Matt. 25:40

TAN BOOKS AND PUBLISHERS, INC.
Rockford, Illinois 61105

Nihil Obstat: Rev. John Roos, S.T.L, J.C.D.
                  Censor Librorum

Imprimatur: ✝ Howard J. Hubbard
                  Bishop of Albany
                  March 25, 1983

Originally published in French in 1974 by Editions S.O.S. of 106, rue du Bac, 75341 Paris, France, under the title *Louise de Marillac ou la Passion du Pauvre Hier et Aujourd'hui.* (ISBN: 02. 7185. 0781. 0).

English translation published by arrangement with Editions S.O.S.

Library of Congress Catalog Card No.: 83-50058

ISBN: 0-89555-215-9

Printed and bound in the United States of America.

TAN BOOKS AND PUBLISHERS, INC.
P.O. Box 424
Rockford, Illinois 61105

1983

TO
THE DAUGHTERS OF CHARITY
OF THE UNITED STATES
PAST AND PRESENT

THE DAUGHTERS OF CHARITY
OF SAINT VINCENT DE PAUL
1633 - 1983

350th ANNIVERSARY EDITION

CONTENTS

Chapter I

EARLY PREPARATION

Nearly 400 years after the birth of Louise de Marillac, the identity of her mother remains unknown. The registers for the years 1591 - 1595 of the parish church of Ferrieres-en-Brie might have shed some light on the matter had they not mysteriously disappeared. Other official documents, however, which are still extant, speak eloquently of this carefully guarded secret. The contract drawn up at the time of her marriage bears cruel witness to the mystery surrounding the birth of the future saint. The cloud under which she was to grow up provided Louise with her first experience of true poverty: that of the child deprived of maternal affection.

There would be some small consolation for the little girl. Her father, Louis de Marillac, loved her dearly. The son of a noble family of Auvergne, he was co-heir of Ferrieres-en-Brie and Farinvilliers. At the time of the birth of Louise, he was an officer in the service of King Henry III. Two years previously he had lost his lawful wife, Marie de la Roziere, who had left him childless after five years of marriage.

Although the mother of Louise would never be identified, Louis de Marillac recognized the child as his own. On August 15, 1591, he bequeathed to her an annual pension of 100 pounds in addition to land at Ferrieres-en-Brie.

Important as the recognition and the financial security would be, they could never compensate for the love of a

1

true mother. Louis de Marillac sought to fill this void when he confided his daughter to the care of the Dominican Nuns at the Royal Monastery of Poissy. It is unclear at what age Louise became a boarder at the convent, but her adult life proves that she received a solid intellectual and religious formation from the nuns. More importantly, it can be supposed that she found a measure of the affection she so greatly needed in one of the religious, her great aunt, Louise de Marillac.

On January 12, 1595, Louis de Marillac married a widow, Antoinette Le Camus Thibaut, who brought four children—three boys and a girl—into his home. Shortly before his second marriage, Louis de Marillac once again provided for his daughter. By a binding notarized statement he bequeathed a pension of thirteen ecus to Louise "because of the deep affection he has always had and continues to have for the beneficiary so as to insure suitable means for her support after the death of the benefactor and to provide the necessary dowry for her future marriage."

A few years later Louis de Marillac would make yet another provision for his "natural daughter." November 23, 1602 he added 1,200 pounds to his bequests to Louise. This gesture was prompted by the fact that on December 28, 1601, Antoinette Le Camus had given birth to a daughter, Innocente. Unfortunately, things were going so badly in the de Marillac household that Louis filed a suit against his wife to prevent the liquidation of their common property. In such a climate his precautions to defend the financial interests of Louise are understandable. In referring to her in his will of 1604 he wrote, "She has been my greatest consolation in this world. She was given to me by God to calm my spirit in the afflictions of life." In this will he added yet another ten ecus of pension to be drawn from the profits of the land at Farinvilliers "for three Masses and for alms for the support of the aforementioned Mademoiselle Louise de Marillac, my daughter."

Two days later, July 25, he died.

Louise was thirteen at the time. Her grief was profound since there had been perfect harmony between her father and herself. If too much stress should not be placed on the affirmation of Gobillon, her future biographer, that Louis de Marillac had taught his daughter philosophy "so as to train her reason and introduce her to advanced sciences," it is nonetheless true that he awakened her intelligence to matters of the spirit.

By placing Louise with her great aunt in the convent of Poissy, Louis de Marillac was certain that she would receive a solid literary and artistic education. Hilarion de la Coste places Louise's Dominican namesake among the outstanding women of the early seventeenth century: "a woman renowned for her wisdom and especially for her piety and possessing a great love for literature and art." Among her other talents she was gifted in Greek and Latin. She translated into verse the *Office of the Blessed Virgin Mary,* the *Psalms,* and the *Canticle of Canticles.* At her school, Louise would be introduced to the most beautiful texts of the Christian tradition. Moreover, other girls of noble families were received at the convent. The nuns, among whom the memory of Louis IX, Saint Louis, still lived, taught their young charges their first lessons of charity toward the poor and the poorest among them—of which the king had given the example by serving them himself, washing their feet and even kissing a leper. All this had occurred centuries earlier, but the young Louise saw it pictured in the stained glass windows and learned it in her history of France. Her teachers did not fail to point out to her that the king had acted thus because he saw Christ present in the poor.

Thus light and shadow alternate during the first years of the life of Louise. She grew into adolescence in the midst of luxury, but there was a void in her heart: her unknown mother, her father's troubled household and finally the

3

death of her father, whom she loved so dearly, after a painful illness.

Another more concrete experience of poverty awaited Louise. Gobillon writes: "When she was sufficiently educated, she was placed in the care of an able and virtuous woman of Paris to learn the tasks suitable to her condition." A wealthy condition? Certainly not. Simply the tasks any woman should know how to perform. Louise herself would speak of this period later. Her mistress is no longer the intellectual Dominican, her great aunt Louise, but "a good, devout woman" who took in other "young women" in order to earn her living. The woman was so poor that the compassionate Louise proposed "taking in work from the merchants" so as to help with the household expenses. She also encouraged other young boarders to do the same. Even so, expenses had to be reduced to a minimum. Since there were no more lay sisters as at Poissy, Louise "undertook the most humble of household tasks such as polishing the floors, tasks normally performed by servants"—and this at a period when there were clear distinctions between master and servant. After the brilliant education of Poissy, Louise de Marillac was brutally initiated into the life of the poor who must work in order to live.

Unfortunately for Louise, the provisions of her father's will were not carried out. Official documents leave no doubt in the matter. The combined pensions and legacies amounted to the then considerable sum of 6,000 pounds, but the "curator of the goods of the aforementioned Mademoiselle Louise de Marillac" was obliged to sue in order to obtain for her the monies her father had left her. A verdict issued at Chatelet, September 7, 1610, obliged her uncle Michel de Marillac, then tutor to her half sister Innocente, to pay her 300 pounds pension, a thirty-pound annuity and back payments.

At the time of the verdict Louise was nineteen. She had been declared legally of age the previous August 13. Fully aware of the legal battle in which she was embroiled, she must have suffered a great deal. At the threshold of her adult life she was to learn that poverty would sometimes necessitate struggle even with the members of one's own family. It would only be through a lengthy court battle that she would finally obtain what was rightfully hers from her uncle Michel, then Counselor to the King.

Louise did not wait until she was twenty to plan for her future. This probably explains why she sought to be declared of age at nineteen and wanted to know exactly what her future means of subsistence would be. She was strongly attracted to the religious life, and at that period, entrance into a convent required a rather substantial dowry.

The early seventeenth century was one of intense religious renewal in France. The de Marillac family would play an important role in this rebirth of religious life. One of Louise's cousins entered the Jesuits, who were re-established in France in 1603. Her uncle Michel was instrumental in bringing the Carmelites onto French territory in 1604, and two of his nieces, cousins of Louise, would be admitted. In 1606 Octavien de Marillac received the Franciscan habit, and August 2 of the same year all of Parisian society assisted at the solemn installation of a new congregation, the Daughters of the Passion, in the capital.

Louise so dreamt of sharing their life of prayer and penance that she engaged herself to do so by vow. But she was told, "That is not the way," by the Provincial of the Capuchins, who assured her that "God has other designs," since the delicacy of her health could never support the austerities of the Daughters of Saint Claire.

In 1607 the Ursulines opened their first house in France, in Paris. The daughter of Michel de Marillac and Louise's half sister Innocente were among their pupils. Louise wondered if God were calling her to join these outstanding educators. At twenty she was troubled by doubt and uncertainty concerning her future. She sought to discover what

God wanted of her.

At that period, the decision of parents was considered to be the expression of the will of God. Louise had no parents, but she was a member of an illustrious family which at that time was at the height of its influence. In 1607 King Henry IV was the witness at the marriage of her father's half brother, Louis de Beaumont, to Catherine de Medicis, aunt of the Queen Mother. Her aunt, Valence, had been married for ten years to Octavien Doni d'Attichy, Minister of the Finances of France. Their home was open to Louise, and it was perhaps they who first introduced her to Antoine Le Gras, secretary of the Queen, Marie de Medicis.

In the seventeenth century the choice for young women was clear: marry or enter a convent. Since the cloister was closed to Louise because of her delicate health, she had to accept marriage. She did so January 15, 1613 in the church of Saint Gervais in Paris. Antoine Le Gras was not a nobleman, thus she became simply "Mademoiselle Le Gras"—a name by which she is sometimes designated even today.

The marriage contract was signed in the Doni d'Attichy home where Louise was residing. It contains a list of the property brought by the bride, including the 6,000-pound legacy which Louise had received from her father. However, her limited finances are apparent since there is no mention of furniture. It adds that "Mademoiselle de Marillac had only her ordinary clothing."

Thus it was that Louise experienced the effects of poverty in the smallest details of her daily existence. She felt the wounds without understanding why God was permitting them. Only later in her life would she see this painful period as a precious introduction into the world of poverty that would enable her to understand the sufferings of the poor.

But the time for that had not yet come. Louise de Marillac was first to pass through a period of peace during which she would discover at least the joy of human love.

Chapter II

WIFE AND MOTHER

At the time of his marriage, Antoine Le Gras was thirty-two; his bride was ten years his junior. The difference in age as well as Louise's aspirations to the religious life have caused some to see this union simply as a "marriage of convenience." There is perhaps some truth in this assertion. However, there are strong indications that a deep love soon grew up between them. The devotion of the young couple was apparent to their contemporaries. A letter from the Bishop of Bellay, who knew Louise intimately, speaks of "your dearly loved husband." Louise seems at last to have found love and security.

By her marriage Louise became a member of the household of the Queen Mother. She was no longer an orphan who was tolerated but scorned. Antoine Le Gras had his place at court and Louise was received there. Although they were not wealthy, they were able to spend the then considerable sum of 18,000 pounds to move their home from the parish of Saint-Merry to the more fashionable rue Courteau-Villain in the parish of Saint-Sauveur.

A son was born to the young couple October 18, 1613. Louise then knew the profound joy of motherhood. Vincent de Paul would later say of her, "I have never known anyone so completely a mother as you." The future seemed bright indeed.

Louise divided her time between her duties as wife and

mother and her responsibilities as a lady of the court. While she attended many glittering receptions, she was careful not to forget God. The poor also had their place in her life. One of her servants recounts, "She brought sweets, preserves, biscuits and other good things to the needy; she cleaned their wounds and vermin; she also prepared their bodies for burial." Her household was so pious that two of her servants left her to enter the religious life.

Louise's piety had a solid doctrinal base which she was careful to maintain. She and her husband had permission, rare at that time, to read the Bible in the Louvain translation. She also participated assiduously in parish activities where she met noblewomen who would later become her collaborators in works of charity.

This untroubled happiness was to prove fragile. The family was visited by death: Octavien Doni d'Attichy in 1614, and his wife three years later. This couple who had opened their hearts and their home to Louise in her time of distress were very dear to her. They had been the witnesses at her marriage, and Valence was the godmother of her son Michel. So it was that the d'Attichy children found devoted protectors in Louise and Antoine, who went so far as to serve their needs to the detriment of their own, without receiving any recompense in return.

This was indeed a cruel loss, but greater sufferings, of which she saw only the first shadows, were soon to strike Louise. Her child would develop slowly despite the care she showered upon him. The first signs of illness appeared in her husband, making him irritable and difficult to live with.

Antoine's illness was unquestionably exacerbated by the political events of the time. As secretary to the Regent, Marie de Medicis, he felt keenly the consequences of the serious dispute between the Queen Mother and the future King Louis XIII. In 1617, after the assassination of her favorite, Concini, she went into exile in Blois. It was apparent that Louis XIII intended to reign alone. The question remained concerning the fate of the household of the Regent. It was a time of anguish for those whose fortunes were tied to hers. And that anguish would become greater yet when, in 1619, Marie de Medicis fled Blois. Louise shared the anxiety of her husband, whose health was worsening.

She sought spiritual support. The Lord would not fail her. In 1618 - 1619 there would be the visits to Paris of "our good father of Geneva," Francis de Sales. His *Introduction to the Devout Life* and *Treatise on the Love of God* would help to sustain Louise during this trying period. One of Francis' disciples, Camus, Bishop of Bellay, whose Advent and Lenten sermons were so well received in Paris, would provide needed spiritual direction through 1623. There was also her close friendship with the Visitation nun, Catherine de Beaumont. Above all, Louise found spiritual strength in her uncle, Michel, against whom she bore no rancor because of his delays in delivering her inheritance.

The correspondence of Louise de Marillac during these years reveals her spiritual anguish caused by the retardation of her son, the illness of her husband and the deprivation of those who had defended her in time of need. She is once again disturbed about her future and wonders just what it is that God is asking of her. At a period when Divine Justice was a major spiritual theme, Louise turned to anxious introspection: death, illness, loss of fortune—was it all a punishment from God for her failure to keep her adolescent vow to enter the cloister?

The spiritual direction that she received at the time would enable Louise to reach at last that poverty of heart which purifies and opens the soul to the Holy Spirit and to the desire to serve the neighbor. The Bishop of Bellay would preach joy to her: "I await the time when serenity will return to you after the storm clouds which have prevented you from seeing the bright joy which fills those who serve God."

Her uncle Michel speaks of abandonment:

> It is well, Mademoiselle, to learn from ex-
> perience that God is not attached to our plans or
> designs, and that those who find Him are those who
> seek Him as He wishes to communicate Himself
> and not as they judge useful or profitable to their
> advancement, since frequently this imagined
> usefulness is only the product of our selfish desires.
> But the poor in spirit, who recognize and
> peacefully accept their poverty, receive everything
> from God as it comes. They are happy to surrender
> themselves to Him and do not seek to prescribe
> what He should do. They accept what comes, make
> use of everything with humility and gratitude, and
> remain always poor in spirit, content to do their
> best without being troubled by their deficiencies
> and weaknesses.

These reassuring, calming words were necessary since
there was a perpetual exchange of decrees of banishment
and treaties of reconciliation between Marie de Medicis
and her son: the Treaty of Angouleme in 1619; the Treaty
of Angers in 1620 following yet another revolt by the
Regent. Throughout this period there were constant cries of
alarm for Louise and for Antoine, whose health continued
to fail.

Ever fearful that her trials were a punishment from God
for her infidelity to Him, the young wife promised the Lord
on May 4, 1623, that she would never remarry should her
husband die. But this did not prove sufficient. Her anguish
continued.

A short time later Louise was plunged into a torment of
self-searching. She describes her anguish:

The following feast of the Ascension, May 25, I

entered a dark night of the soul which would last until Pentecost. I was tortured with doubt about whether or not I should leave my husband, as I believed I ought, so as to make up for my first vow and have greater liberty to serve God and my neighbor.

I feared that my attachment to my director would prevent me from accepting another, although I felt that I should do so. I suffered from doubts concerning the immortality of my soul, and this doubt led me to question Divinity itself. These three doubts gripped my soul in unimaginable pain.

Shadows, powerlessness, the total poverty of a soul tottering on the edge of despair! God Himself would come to her aid on June 4, 1623, during the Mass for the feast of Pentecost, in the church of Saint-Nicolas-des-Champs. Louise herself describes the experience:

In an instant my spirit was cleared of all its doubts. I was advised that I should remain with my husband; that a time would come when I would be in a situation to make vows of poverty, chastity and obedience; and that I would be with other persons who would do the same thing. I understood that I would be in a place where I would be able to help my neighbor, but I did not see how this could be since there would be much coming and going.

I was also assured that I should be at peace concerning my director, that God would give me one whom He seemed to show me. I found it repugnant to accept him; nevertheless, I acquiesced. It seemed to me that this change would not take place immediately.

My third doubt was removed by the assurance I

11

felt within me that God was speaking to me, and that since there was a God, I could not doubt the rest.

The whole future life of Louise de Marillac is foreshadowed in these few lines.

Two years later Louise, who had remained constantly at her husband's side, assisted at Antoine Le Gras' last agony. She writes:

> I was alone to assist him in this all-important passing. He showed great devotion until his last sigh. His spirit was entirely attached to God. He repeated over and over to me, "Pray to God for me since I can no longer do so." These words will be forever engraved on my heart.

Louise would never forget her beloved husband whom God called to Himself December 23, 1625. Every year she would have a Mass celebrated for him on the anniversary of his death.

As for herself, Louise was about to experience yet another form of poverty: widowhood.

Chapter III

INITIAL CONSECRATION

Antoine Le Gras left his widow and young son with very limited financial resources. His long illness had prevented him from amassing a fortune. Moreover, as Louise herself tells us, "He devoted so much time and energy to the affairs of the d'Attichy family that he neglected his own." This was all the more serious since at this period there were no retirement plans or life insurance policies. Remuneration was based strictly on services rendered. Louise had to rely on the annuities mentioned in her marriage contract to support her son and herself. These were certainly insufficient to support the way of life to which she had become accustomed in the fashionable Marais district where she lived. She was obliged to move.

Louise would have considerable difficulty in finding a suitable home. Since a move was necessary, she wanted to be nearer to Vincent de Paul, principal of the College of the Bons Enfants, who was now her spiritual director. In 1626 we find her on the rue Saint-Victor but at several different addresses—one the property of a certain Mr. Tiron Saint-Priest, and another belonging to an accountant, Mr. Guerin. On October 12, 1631, Vincent informed her that Mr. Guerin needed his apartment and that once again she would have to move.

At the same time, her son Michel was growing up. He had reached an age when he had a great need for a male influence in his life. In June 1627, after a period of reflection, Louise decided to place him in a seminary which Father Bourdoise had opened in the parish of Saint-Nicolas-du-Chardonnet. It was not far from her home but far enough to create the necessary separation. Would Michel be a priest one day? His mother certainly hoped so, and Michel, at least at this period, does not seem to be opposed.

Louise thus found herself alone with a good deal of free time. This she would carefully organize, providing for periods of prayer, work and social activities. In the "Rule of Life" that she drew up for herself at this time, there is a provision for two retreats a year which would end with practical resolutions. She left nothing to chance in her desire to reach Christian perfection.

At a period when Louise was struggling financially, her family—particularly her uncles—was enjoying great royal favor. Michel became Minister of Finances in 1624 and was reconfirmed in the position in 1626. Louis would soon be Field Marshal of France. Both would be at the side of the King during the siege of La Rochelle. Louis XIII is quoted as saying, "Would that my whole council were composed of Marillacs."

How great a contrast existed between this rise to prominence of her family and the relative poverty of the young widow of Antoine Le Gras. Louise undoubtedly accepted privations so as to provide properly for her growing son. However, there was a greater, deeper spiritual motivation. She would grow to love poverty because of her ever-increasing intimacy with Jesus Christ, who was becoming "All" in her life. She wrote:

> I must imitate Jesus as a bride seeks to conform herself to her spouse . . .
> Being rich, He chose holy poverty. I begged Him, with all my heart, to grant me the grace to imitate Him, hoping that, after having given myself

to Him for so long in desire, I might finally do so in
deed.

These words are recorded in her retreat notes of 1625 -
1633. A careful reading of them shows that Louise did not
immediately attain that poverty of spirit which leads to total
abandonment into the hands of God. The death of her husband, her son's entry into the seminary, and separation
from her family produced a climate of solitude in which she
would once again question the meaning of her life. Her
writings of this period contain repeated protestations of her
desire to give herself entirely to God. We read: "I have
resolved that on every doubtful occasion I will seek to know
what the Son of God would have done in like circumstances." Elsewhere: "I must willingly make Jesus the
unique possessor of my soul as He is already its master."
And: "I will abandon myself into the hands of God."

However, she already felt called to serve her neighbor.
Her "Rule of Life" clearly shows this: "I will try not to be
lazy, but to keep busy working cheerfully for the Church,
for the poor or for my household." Her retreat notes show
the spiritual motivation for her service:

> To give myself to God to serve my neighbor in a
> condition in which I may be subject to blame, im-
> itating Our Lord in His conversations with sinners
> and in His entire life, during the course of which
> He despised His personal interests for the good of
> His creatures. This is what I desire to do if it be His
> holy will.

Vincent de Paul, who had probably entered Louise's life
a year or two before the death of her husband, followed the
spiritual quest of the young widow, helping her to discern
the will of God. This quest would lead both of them very
far.

St. Louise as a young woman. This portrait is in the possession of the de Marillac's descendants.

Chapter IV

FRIENDSHIP IN THE LORD

No one seems to know just where or when Vincent de Paul and Louise de Marillac first met. The parish of Clichy where Vincent had been named pastor in 1612 was on de Marillac land. Moreover, his position as tutor in the de Gondi household had put him in contact with the high society of the period and especially with its spiritual leaders, not least among whom was Louise's uncle, Michel de Marillac. The de Gondi residence in Paris was in the parish of Saint-Sauveur, rue Pavee, where Louise lived from 1615 to 1626. In addition, one of her closest friends was Catherine de Beaumont whom Vincent had installed as Superior of the Visitation in 1622.

A meeting was therefore very possible, although the exact circumstances cannot be established. Louise's Pentecost experience of 1623 may also be considered as the beginning of their relationship. The first letter of Vincent de Paul to Louise de Marillac is dated October 30, 1626. Her first letter to him was written June 5, 1627. Both of these letters show that the young widow was already turning to the service of the poor. However, for the time being, the ever-wise Vincent de Paul was satisfied with encouraging her to make small gestures of material help in their regard.

Vincent awaited a sign of the divine will while constantly placing the example of Jesus Christ before her eyes. Moreover, he wanted her decision to be entirely personal.

"The Holy Spirit will be your rule and your guide," he told her.

However, none of Louise's concerns was unimportant to Vincent, especially her worries about her son, who was such a source of preoccupation for her. Michel was constantly wavering in his "vocation." His fervor had so clearly diminished that he had to withdraw from the seminary. This was a painful disappointment for his mother. Vincent wrote to her January 17, 1628:

> What can I say to you about your son? Just as it was unwise to place too much confidence in his first attraction to the priesthood, so now you should not be overly upset about his seeming rejection of it. Leave the matter entirely to the will or the non-will of Our Lord. It is for Him to direct young souls. He has greater concern for Michel than you can since he belongs more to Him than to you.

There are few letters from Vincent to Louise which do not mention the unstable Michel. After leaving the seminary, he became a day student at Saint-Nicolas, residing either with his mother, or in her absence, with Vincent. In 1631 we find him at the Jesuit Lycee Louis-le-Grand. Louise would continue to worry about her son until his long-delayed marriage, July 14, 1651, which brought with it a position in the Treasury. Vincent had also provided a position for him as magistrate for Saint-Lazare in charge of justice on lands which the Congregation of the Mission had acquired after its union with the Canons of Saint-Victor.

Louise would be constantly sustained by Vincent de Paul as she moved along the path toward confidence in and surrender to God. He wrote, "Be cheerful . . . Honor the inactivity and the hidden life of the Son of God . . . Submit to the will of God in time of difficulty . . . Adore Divine Providence, follow it, do not anticipate it." These words were to form the recurring theme of their correspondence at this period. In the trials that were to follow, they would prove necessary. Louise, who had had little contact with her family during the era of their great prestige, would be closely united to them when misfortune struck.

In 1629 Michel de Marillac as Keeper of the Seal had published the Code Michau, an ordinance of 461 articles touching all areas of public administration. However, his rift with the Prime Minister, Cardinal Richelieu, grew ever wider, empoisoned yet further by the intrigues of the Queen Mother, Marie de Medicis. When Louis XIII decided to place all his trust in the Cardinal, the ruin of the de Marillacs was rapid. Michel was obliged to relinquish the seal and was imprisoned at Chateaudun on January 12, 1631. He died there August 7, 1632.

Louis de Marillac, Marshall of France, was arrested October 30, 1630 on the battlefield of Felizzo in Piedmont. On May 8, 1632, by a supreme irony, he heard a sentence of death pronounced against him in the very terms of the ordinance drawn up by his brother. He was executed the following day on the Place de Greve in keeping with Article 344 of Volume II of the Code Michau.

Vincent de Paul knew how greatly these events had afflicted the niece of the two outstanding members of the de Marillac family. In vain had Louis de Marillac's wife, daughter of Cosme de Medicis and aunt of the Queen Mother, tried to gain the mercy of the Cardinal. Fruitless likewise was the intervention of Madame de Combalet, the future Duchess of Aiguillon and niece of Richelieu. Louise herself considered trying to help, but Vincent warned her, "Be careful not to become too deeply involved." He would nevertheless try to console her. When Louis' wife died in September 1631, he wrote:

The Son of God wept over Lazarus; why would

you not grieve for this good woman? There is no harm in this provided that, like the Son of God, you conform yourself to the will of the Father. I am certain you will do so.

The week after Louis was executed, Vincent once again comforted her while urging her to submit to the will of God:

What you tell me of the fate of the Marshal seems worthy of compassion and deeply afflicts me. Let us honor in this the good pleasure of God and the happiness of those who honor the suffering of the Son of God by their own. It is not important how our relatives go to God provided they do so. And the good use of this manner of death is one of the surest means to attain eternal life. Therefore, let us not pity him but let us together submit to the adorable will of God.

The will of God! The ardent soul of Louise de Marillac sought to discern clearly the designs of the Almighty in her life at this period when widowhood afforded her more freedom of action. She desired with all her being to give herself to God, but she did not as yet see what direction she should take. She wrote, "In my idleness, the days seem like months to me. I want to await calmly God's good time."

Yes, she wanted to be at peace while awaiting the manifestation of the will of God, but she was obliged constantly to renew her good intentions as Vincent advised her:

Do not feel that all is lost because of the revolt you experience interiorly. It has rained hard. The thunder has crashed. Is the weather any less beautiful because of that? Let tears flood your heart and demons thunder within you as much as they will. Be assured that you are not, for all that, less dear to Our Lord. Live, then, in the security of His love.

When Louise found herself the object of malicious gossip, Vincent compassionated her. He told her:

> How I suffer in your time of suffering! But why be disturbed? Such is the order of Providence. What real harm have you to fear? This man says that you promised to marry him and it is not true. You are unjustly criticized. You are suffering without cause. Are you afraid of what others are saying of you? So be it! But remember that this is one of the surest means possible in this life for conforming yourself to the Son of God.

Nevertheless, Vincent de Paul came to realize that only meaningful activity would prevent the young widow from turning in on herself. It was precisely at this time that he needed someone to visit and encourage the associations of lay workers which, since 1617, he had founded wherever he had preached missions. And so he sent Louise.

It was high adventure for a young woman to travel the highways of France, which in that era were anything but safe. She used coaches, horses or boats as necessity demanded, paying little attention to her personal comfort. But Vincent no longer hesitated. The needs of the poor of the countryside and the good of Louise herself urged him to send her out. Moreover, Louise was at last certain that God was speaking to her and leading her. She was "ready to give herself to the service of her neighbor under the conditions and on the occasions which God would present to her."

A 17th-century Daughter of Charity carrying bread and soup to the poor.

Chapter V

JOURNEYS OF CHARITY

"Go in the name of the Lord, Mademoiselle." It was thus that Vincent de Paul wrote to Louise de Marillac on May 6, 1629. Her long period of waiting was over. Her life as a dedicated servant of the poor had begun.

Vincent knew well the difficulties she would encounter. He urged her to look beyond the human to the example of the life of Jesus Christ. He instructed her:

> You will receive Holy Communion on the day of your departure so as to honor the charity of Our Lord and the journeys that He made for this very purpose. Accept, in imitation of Him, the sufferings, contradictions, fatigue and labor that you will meet so that it may please Him to bless your trip, to give you His spirit and the grace to act in keeping with that spirit, and to endure your sufferings in the manner in which He endured His.

In response to his urgings, Louise renewed the gift of herself to Christ and to His poor. She wrote:

> No more resistance to Jesus . . . No more thoughts but in Jesus . . . No more actions but for Jesus . . . No longer to live but for Jesus and my neighbor so that, in this unifying love, I may love

all that Jesus loved, and in this core of love, which is the eternal love of God for His creatures, I may obtain the graces that His mercy wills to bestow upon me . . .

The first of the Confraternities of Charity which Louise would be sent to visit had been established in 1617 in the parish of Chatillon-les-Dombes where, for a brief period, Vincent de Paul had been pastor. In subsequent years, as Vincent's missionary work expanded, similar groups were set up in parishes across France. They were composed of women, and occasionally men, who met to determine how they could alleviate the misery of the poor of the region. So that their charitable activity would be more than a passing gesture, Vincent provided a minimal structure for the associations and defined the role of each member. The entire work was placed under one guiding principle: *The poor are Jesus Christ.*

The associations were self-governing. The members elected officers, set up conditions for membership and determined the manner in which the poor were to be served. Their rules, drawn up by Vincent himself, reveal an admirable compassion and respect for the person of the poor. We read:

> The Servant of the Poor [as the members were called] will care for the sick as if she were caring for her own child, and should the patient die, she will attend the funeral, taking the place of a mother who accompanies her child to the grave.

Minute details of care can be found in the Rules of the Confraternities. Yet they were flexible enough to meet changing needs and situations. In some areas collections were taken up to meet the needs of the poor; in others, sheep were raised to defray expenses. Everywhere personal service was required. There was always direct contact with the poor who were treated with gentleness, respect and devotedness. The Rule states:

> The Servant of the Poor responsible for days shall prepare the noon meal and bring it to the sick whom she shall greet cheerfully and charitably . . . She shall accomplish her task with love as if she were caring for her own son, or, better, God Himself, since He considers the good done for the poor as being done to Him . . . She shall try to raise the spirits of the sick . . .

With the passage of time, however, good will began to weaken. Abuses crept in. In one area, visits became less and less frequent. In another, the treasurer accumulated funds rather than spend them for the poor. In yet another place, no accounts were kept at all. Numerous other problems had arisen in the ten years since Vincent had founded the Confraternity of Chatillon. When he and his priests returned to the places where they had preached missions and established charitable associations, they saw that the zeal of the members needed to be rekindled. Who was better qualified to do this than Louise de Marillac? Her time was her own. She had a great desire to share her love of God with others. Moreover, she possessed an extraordinary talent for organization coupled with prudence and good judgment. And so Vincent sent her *"in nomine Domini."*

She took him at his word. Concerning her trip to Saint-Cloud she wrote:

> I left on the feast of Saint Agatha, February 5, 1630. At the time of Holy Communion that morning it seemed to me that Our Lord was inspiring me to give myself entirely to Him and to receive Him as a spouse. I felt myself deeply united to God by

this desire which was unusual for me. I felt called to leave all to follow my Spouse, to consider Him ever after as such, and to look upon the difficulties which I would surely encounter as coming from His goodness.

Saint-Cloud, however, was not her first trip. She had been traveling throughout the countryside for better than a year visiting the Confraternities at Asnieres, Argenteuil, Sannois, Franconville, Herblay, Conflans and Montmirail, to name but a few. After each visit she sent a precise evaluation of the work to Vincent:

Sannois: No destitute but the small land owners are so debt-ridden that they are in danger of dying of starvation since they are unable to sell their possessions.

Franconville: The treasurer gives a small sum to the poor to meet their own needs, thus personal service has been lost.

Conflans: Funds are hoarded and the poor are deprived of necessities.

Herblay: All goes well. The poor are served with great zeal.

Vincent studied all these reports and used them to make necessary changes in the Confraternities which were now scattered across the French countryside. Soon they would be established in Paris itself where each parish desired one. The parishes of Saint-Sauveur, Saint-Nicolas-du-Chardonnet, Saint-Eustache, Saint-Sulpice and Saint-Merry were among the first. The wealthy vied with one another to become members. Soon the court of Louis XIII became involved. In 1634, 120 noblewomen formed the Confraternity of the Hotel-Dieu of Paris.

Vincent de Paul and Louise de Marillac collaborated

closely in this growing work of charity. They stood together in success and failure. And all did not go well. Sometimes opposition came from local authorities both civil and religious. In Beauvais, where there was unrest among the beggars, Vincent's undertaking troubled the representative of the King. In Montreuil there was need for reorganization. Vincent himself went to visit the Confraternity and later sent Louise to adapt the charter to meet local needs. All their efforts proved fruitless. The same thing happened in Chalons. Vincent had given Louise a letter of introduction to the local pastor. However, the Bishop, unaware of what had been going on, questioned her concerning her plans. Despite her explanation, he remained unconvinced of the necessity for the work and she was obliged to leave. Throughout it all, Vincent supported and encouraged his collaborator. Moreover, he seemed concerned that she was overextending herself. He counselled her:

> Be careful not to overdo it . . . The spirit of God leads us on gently to do the good which we can reasonably accomplish so that we can do it consistently and for a longer period of time. Act thus, Mademoiselle, and you will be acting according to the spirit of God.

The beginnings in Beauvais had been particularly difficult, but finally opposition gave way to enthusiastic acceptance and Louise received a joyous welcome. Sharing her pleasure, Vincent de Paul wrote:

> When you are honored and esteemed, unite your heart to the heart of the Son of God when He was mocked, despised and badly treated. A truly humble person abases herself as much in honor as in contempt, just as the bee gathers honey from the dew whether it falls on wormwood or a rose.

He advised obedience when Louise was faced with the opposition of the Bishop of Chalons:

> Offer to make any changes in the charter which he deems necessary, and even to leave if he would prefer that. Such is the true spirit of God. You must look upon the Bishop as the interpreter of the will of God in the present situation. Thus you will imitate the humility of the Son of God in the accomplishment of good.

Undaunted, Louise set out again. She went to Senlis, Soissons, Meaux and Chartres, lodging where and as she could. At Verneuil she stayed with the baker's family; at Pont-Sainte-Maxence, it was at the Fleur de Lys Inn.

Charity had set her free. She exclaimed, "I feel so well that this trip causes me to want to do nothing other than travel the length and breadth of the countryside, *provided the poor be better served.*"

The zeal of Louise reveals much more than the natural activity of an ardent soul. Her desire that "the poor be better served" was a response to the call of the suffering Christ. She sought to help the poor to discover, in their misery, the loving, watchful tenderness of God, "since each of us in particular is called to be His beloved."

Louise's delicate health showed her her own limitations but it did not deter her. She describes one particularly difficult journey:

> I left for Ansiere on Wednesday of the Christmas Ember Days. Don't laugh! You can imagine the trip in the dead of winter. I had been a little fearful about undertaking it because of my ailments, but I felt fortified by the awareness that I was doing so in a spirit of obedience. At Holy Communion, on the day of my departure, I made an act of faith. These

sentiments remained with me for a long time. I felt that God would give me the necessary strength so long as I trusted that He was able to sustain me despite all appearances. I believed that He would do so if I recalled the faith that enabled Saint Peter to walk on the water. All during my trip I seemed to be carried along, consoled in the belief that God, despite my unworthiness, wanted me to help my neighbor to arrive at the knowledge of Him.

Every human distress became for Louise de Marillac a call of God to the better service of the poor. She kept before her eyes the words of Saint Irenaeus: "If the glory of God is man fully alive, the life of man is the vision of God."

St. Louise instructing little girls. This painting is in the provincial house in Havana, Cuba.

Chapter VI

AT THE SERVICE OF THE POOR

After her bitter experience of personal poverty, Louise de Marillac grew ever more sensitive to the misery of mankind. Her compassionate heart was open to the poor of the countryside, to the victims of the greed and cunning of the rich, to the lonely, the sick, the old and the rejected. She traveled throughout France for five years on foot, on horseback, by coach and by boat. Confronted by a sea of suffering, she reflected on the means for bringing about a "better service of the poor."

Her visits to the Confraternities had taught her that volunteers, however great their good will, were not enough. There was a need for persons who would "always" be available. Vincent de Paul shared her views. Together they waited. Their confidence would not prove vain.

As Vincent and his priests went about preaching missions, young girls would occasionally approach them expressing a desire to serve God with their whole being. These simple, upright peasants came from villages such as Suresnes, Colombes and Argenteuil. Vincent understood quickly that they would need able assistance if they were to persevere in the service of the poor which they had first undertaken alongside the members of the Confraternities of Charity. He could find no more capable collaborator to train them than Louise de Marillac.

One among them would show the way: Marguerite

Naseau of Suresnes. Her story is too beautiful not to repeat as Vincent himself told it. For him she was the prototype of the yet unthought of Daughter of Charity:

> Marguerite Naseau, of Suresnes, was the first sister who had the happiness of pointing out the road to our other sisters, both in the education of young girls and in nursing the sick, although she had no other master or mistress but God. She was a poor, uneducated cowherd. Moved by a powerful inspiration from Heaven, the idea occurred to her that she would instruct children, and so she bought an alphabet. But as she could not go to school for instruction, she went and asked the parish priest or curate to tell her what were the first four letters of the alphabet. On another occasion, she asked what were the next four, and so on for the rest. Afterward, whilst she minded her cows, she studied her lesson. If she saw anyone passing by who seemed to know how to read, she would say, "Sir, how is this word pronounced?" And so little by little she learned to read, and she then taught the other girls of her village. She afterward made up her mind to go from village to village instructing the young, accompanied by two or three girls whom she had taught.
>
> . . . when she learned that there was a Confraternity of Charity in Paris for the sick poor, she went there, moved by a desire to be employed in this work; and although she greatly desired to continue instructing the young, nevertheless she laid aside this charitable work to take up that of nursing the sick poor, which she believed to be more perfect and necessary. This was, indeed, the will of God, for He intended her to be the first Daughter of Charity and servant of the sick poor of the city of

Paris. She attracted other girls to the work ...
Everybody loved her because there was nothing in
her that was not lovable. Her charity was so great
that she died from sharing her bed with a poor
plague-stricken girl. When she was attacked by
fever, she bade good-bye to the sister who was with
her, as if she had foreseen she was about to die, and
went to the hospital of St. Louis, her heart filled
with joy.

After Marguerite came Marie, Michelle, another
Marguerite, Barbe and Marthe. Louise de Marillac came to
live with them on the rue Fosses-Saint-Victor. It was here
that she added to her vow of widowhood a vow to serve
these girls and to help them to become "good Christians"
dedicated to the corporal and spiritual service of the poor
wherever they were to be found. Other young village girls
would come to join the first arrivals. They would be twelve
in 1634. Thus it was that the Daughters of Charity were
born.

In 1635 France declared war on Spain. Champagne,
Burgundy and Picardy were devastated. In 1636 Paris itself
was threatened by the Croatians, the Hungarians and the
Poles. Two provinces fell into Spanish hands and civil war
broke out in the Southwest. War brought with it numerous
other ills: disease, hunger, devastation by soldiers who
compensated for a lack of pay by pillaging mercilessly.

The hour had not yet come for the Daughters of Charity
to take their place on the battlefield. That was still a few
years in the future. But they did begin to look beyond the
limits of Paris toward the provinces. The beginnings would
be small. In 1637 two sisters went to Richelieu to visit the
sick and instruct poor little girls. Little by little the work
was spreading. In the meantime, another form of poverty
was calling for their attention in Paris: the foundlings.

The work of sheltering abandoned children was not new.

"La Couche," a house run by a woman and her two servants, had been accepting them for some time. However, Vincent de Paul would attest to the Ladies of Charity in 1649 that over a period of fifty years, "not one" had survived.

The parish of Louise de Marillac was near the Port Saint-Landry. Her attention was attracted by what she saw and the terrible things she heard concerning the infants at La Couche. The abuse shocked her. She certainly related her fears to Vincent, who would later say when speaking of the children, "They are even sold to beggars who starve them and break their arms and legs so as to obtain alms."

The Ladies of Charity were called upon for assistance in 1635. However, a full year of negotiations would be necessary before Vincent could inform Louise that it was time to begin. He wrote:

> It was decided at the last meeting (of the Ladies of Charity) that you should be asked to undertake the work with the foundlings provided they can be fed with cow's milk. You could start with two or three.

Louise did not believe that the children should remain at La Couche. After a period of experimentation during which she kept them with her on the rue Saint-Victor and at La Chapelle, her view prevailed. The Ladies rented a house on the rue des Boulangers where twelve children were accepted for care. Louise spent a week there organizing the work. She would continue to visit it regularly. Despite the numerous problems which arose, in 1640 the Ladies decided no longer to place any limitations on the scope of the work and confided to Louise the responsibility for *all* the foundlings of Paris.

The sisters of the young community showed great creativity in caring for the children. Vincent encouraged them in their work, revealing to them the beauty of their task in words which move us even today:

> These children belong to God in a very special way because they have been abandoned by their mothers and fathers. Since they have been created by the all-powerful God, you can be certain that you will never offend Him by loving them too much. They are His children whom you care for for love of Him. I am certain that you have a deep affection for them. Oh, I assure you, you cannot have too much.

Religious art frequently shows Vincent de Paul in the snow with an infant wrapped in his cloak. There is no historical evidence that such a thing ever occurred, but the portrait reveals the truth concerning his deep affection for these abandoned children. He could not see one without trying to help as the following note to Louise demonstrates: "Would you take a foundling which a noble couple brought to me yesterday? He was found in a field two or three days ago."

The house on the rue des Boulangers was quickly too small to provide for the needs of all these children. Faced with the ever-growing number of infants, Louise de Marillac was obliged to create a whole new method of child care. Her response was to establish, for the first time in France, a program of foster care.

March 30, 1640, the first four infants were confided to wet nurses in the country. The selection process was rigorous. Foster mothers had to furnish references not only from the pastor of the village church who attested to their moral character, but also from a doctor who evaluated their general health and the quality of their milk. The whole method was rare in the seventeenth century, and it served as a model for the future care, both public and religious, of abandoned children.

Nineteen more children were placed the first month, and as the work expanded, many more were added. In September 1642 Sister Jeanne, from the parish of Saint-Germain in Paris, was sent to ascertain the progress of the children placed in Normandy.

Once again, after a daring initiative, we see a careful work of organization. The minute concern for the well-being of the children on the part of both Vincent and Louise is evidenced by the fact that, despite their multiple responsibilities, the registers for the work are in their handwriting. Moreover, records were kept on each child: age, sex, observations made during the visit concerning the infant's health, the quality of care, etc. One report states, "The 400 children in Normandy are much better cared for than the 232 in Picardy. Ten had to be moved and placed with foster mothers who would take better care of them." In 1643 Vincent de Paul estimated that 1,200 children had been cared for under the program in a period of five years.

The civil war would greatly trouble this work. There was little or no money to pay the foster mothers who often brought the children back to the sisters. Louise was forced to borrow money to meet expenses, but even this was insufficient. Gobillon, the first biographer of Louise de Marillac, tells us that she and the first sisters "deprived themselves even of necessities to increase funds . . . They ate but one meager meal a day." As early as 1644, the annual cost of caring for abandoned infants had risen to 40,000 pounds.

The ever-increasing number of foundlings confided to them pushed the sisters to new initiatives. In 1645 the weaned children were placed at Bicetre in Paris, although Louise was well aware of the difficulties that would arise because of the war. She managed to get a supply of wheat through the battle lines, but once she had it, the sisters had to improvise ovens to bake the bread. Moreover, despite the protests of the wine merchants, they began making and selling wine to meet expenses. And so it was that the work continued.

As for the newborns, they remained for several years at the motherhouse where twelve sisters and a number of wet nurses cared for them. To improve their care, an infant home, the first in France, was built in 1645. It consisted of thirteen cottages surrounding a service area. The Vincentian community had purchased the land, "the Saint-Laurent field in the Saint-Denis district," for the construction. Once the institution was built, the Vincentians rented it to the Ladies of Charity for the foundlings. In 1654 Louise asked that the work be extended to accept infants whose mothers had died at the Hotel-Dieu or who were unable to provide for them.

The cost of this service of the foundlings continued to rise. Despite an occasional royal donation, Louise often cried out desperately for help:

> We can no longer, in good conscience, be unmoved by the plight of the foster mothers. They are asking only what is their due in recompense for their labor and for the personal money which they spent for the children. They are now faced with starvation. They sometimes have to come two or three times and each time they leave empty-handed.

The situation was equally grave at the motherhouse. A desperate Louise wrote to Vincent:

> We have seven infants who refuse a bottle and we have only two nurses. Moreover, we do not have a sou to place them in foster care. We are nearly out of bedding and clothing. We can no longer hope to borrow the necessary money. In the

37

name of God, I ask you, if in conscience we can leave these children to die. As for the Ladies of Charity, we are receiving nothing from them.

Vincent would succeed in rekindling the zeal of the Ladies of Charity as only he could. In one of his most celebrated appeals to them, he said:

> If you abandon these little ones what will God say, since it is He who has called you to care for them. The children themselves will cry out, "If you, who are so good, abandon us, it is as if God Himself has abandoned us and is no longer our God."
>
> Their life and their death are in your hands. They will live if you continue your charitable care of them. They will just as surely perish if you abandon them. No one will raise a finger to prevent them from dying. I will now ask for a vote. The time has come to decide their fate.

The Ladies of Charity promised to help and they were true to their word.

Until the end of their lives Vincent de Paul and Louise de Marillac devoted themselves to the care of these "little ones fallen from the nest." Three months before her death, Louise wrote to Vincent:

> For a long time now you have sought ways of helping the children. I beg Our Lord to reveal His holy will in this matter as He does in all others and to grant us the grace of carrying it out faithfully.

To the very end, they would seek together to provide "better service" for the poor abandoned children.

In the meantime, another call—less appealing, certainly,

38

but equally poignant—was raised: the cry of the galley slaves.

The royal prisons were truly the antechambers of Hell. No one knew this better than Vincent de Paul, who had been named Royal Chaplain of the Galleys in 1619. Three years after his appointment he rented a house for a few of the prisoners, hoping to alleviate some of the miseries they suffered at the Conciergerie. However, this small beginning did not satisfy him. In 1632 he took over an abandoned building near the Saint-Bernard Gate to lodge more of them. But the facility was not enough. Funds were needed and it soon became obvious that these could be obtained only from private donations. Vincent thus wrote to Louise de Marillac, in whose parish the shelter was located, to ask her to raise them:

> Charity to these poor prisoners is of incompara-
> ble merit before God. You have done a good thing
> in assisting them. Continue as you have been pro-
> ceeding until I have the opportunity to see you.
> Consider whether or not your Confraternity of
> Charity of Saint-Nicolas would be willing to un-
> dertake the work at least for a while. You could
> help these poor suffering souls with any excess
> funds you might have. What am I saying? I know
> what a difficult task I am placing upon you. I
> thought I would just mention it and let you decide.

As President of the Ladies of Charity of her parish, Louise was able to interest the other members in this work. Their efforts were soon well known. In 1639 a rich banker left Vincent a legacy of 60,000 pounds to be used in the assistance of prisoners. This permitted him to place the Daughters of Charity in their service. Their task was "to serve corporally and spiritually, in sickness and in health, the poor prisoners held in Paris until they leave for the galleys." Their service was very humble: cleaning, washing and cooking. Every day they brought food to the cells, where they were helped by the guards if the burden was too heavy.

It is difficult today to appreciate the daring involved in this undertaking. Louise, however, was very well aware of the danger in which she and Vincent were placing these simple, strong, young country girls by sending them among men whom suffering and remorse had made terribly aggressive and demanding. She would advise the sisters assigned to this work to "renew their spirit of purity and modesty so as to be fortified against the insolence which is to be expected of persons reduced to the state of prisoners." She also urged them "not to listen to their vulgar language."

Louise knew the danger but she was unafraid, certain that "charity will be their best defense." She insisted that if the sisters were circumspect and kind they would "give these poor unfortunate beings little cause to complain of them." She added that they should not converse with the galley slaves "without great necessity, being careful to win them over by meekness and compassion, always bearing in mind the pitiable state to which they are reduced." Vincent himself had said earlier, "I have seen these poor creatures treated like animals, abandoned into the hands of those who have no pity for them."

The Rules for the sisters assigned to this work stressed the spiritual aspect of their service:

> Those who are called by God to this holy employment should be encouraged to have great confidence in Our Lord Jesus Christ, since by serving these poor creatures they are rendering a service to Him who looks upon it as done to Himself. Consequently, He will never fail to give them the grace to overcome the difficulties they may encounter.

But the work was even more difficult than the founders had foreseen. The prisoners were numerous and from every conceivable background. The sisters were advised to find the needed strength in God. The Rule stated:

> Several times a day they will say a special prayer to the Holy Spirit to purify their thoughts, words and actions, particularly at the time of temptations to impurity, should any arise. Thus they will be like the rays of the sun which continually pass over refuse without being contaminated by it.

Did the reality correspond to the ideal presented by the founders? The correspondence of the period would lead us to believe so. Sister Jeanne Luce wrote:

> I worked with Sister Barbe Angiboust in the service of the galley slaves. She showed great patience in putting up with the abuse caused by the ill humor of these poor creatures. Although they were sometimes so angry with her that they threw the soup and meat on the ground and screamed whatever obscenities came to their minds, she never responded. She simply picked everything up cheerfully and calmly as if they had said and done nothing. Moreover, five or six times she prevented the guards from striking them.

The most difficult time for the sisters came when the prisoners were ready to be sent to Marseille for the galleys. The journey was a slow, painful one for these men who would be chained together like animals. To ease their misery Louise asked that shirts and underclothing be distributed to them. The sisters were more than willing, but money was in short supply even for necessities. Louise was forced to admit:

Yesterday our sister who is employed with the galley slaves came to me in tears because she had no more bread to give to these poor creatures. The cost of bread has greatly increased her bill to the baker. She begs and borrows wherever she can to find the means to help them.

However, none of this seems to have dampened the zeal of these dedicated young women. Of Sister Fare, of the parish of Saint-Roch, it was said:

She procured all the help for the prisoners that charity could afford them. She treated the guards and others responsible for these afflicted souls with great prudence, thus almost forcing them to behave more humanely. She would even fall on her knees before them to prevent them from mistreating their charges. In all truth she could say, "I dearly love our poor galley slaves whom I have the honor to serve."

In this arduous work which was undertaken with compassion and respect for the imprisoned, Louise and her companions had found another effective way to insure "the better service" of the poor.

But even this did not satisfy the zeal of their young hearts. They sought yet other poor to serve. So it was that they turned toward the sick, who had been the primary concern of Vincent de Paul when he preached his missions in the countryside of France and established the lay associations of the Confraternities of Charity. In the bylaws of the association we read:

The Confraternity of Charity has been instituted to honor its patron, Our Lord Jesus Christ, and His Holy Mother and to assist corporally and spiritually the sick poor of the places where they are established.

Louise shared this concern of Vincent from the earliest days of their relationship when she visited the Confraternities to see how the service of the sick was being carried out. The first Daughters of Charity were, in reality, "permanent volunteers" in the associations. The Rule of 1645 states, "Their principal end is to serve the sick poor." Jean Francois de Gondi, Archbishop of Paris, spells out the motivation behind this service in the Act of Approbation of the Company:

> It has pleased God to bless this pious and praiseworthy undertaking to such an extent that not only is it established in many towns and villages but also in the principal parishes of the city of Paris.

He then continues:

> Since the members of the Confraternities could not themselves accomplish the lowly tasks necessary for the service of the poor, our dearly beloved Vincent de Paul judged it advisable . . . to assemble some good girls and widows from the country whom God had inspired to dedicate themselves to the service of the sick poor. For several years now they have been engaged in this humble toil, giving edification to those who see them and consolation to the sick.

Vincent recruited the girls. Louise trained them. Then, under the direction of the Ladies of Charity, these young sisters went joyously to serve the sick poor of the parishes. It would be the Ladies of Charity who would draw the attention of Louise and Vincent to the plight of the sick in the Hotel-Dieu of Paris. Gobillon tells us:

> During their visits to the hospital Mademoiselle Le Gras and some other pious noblewomen had noticed that the sick poor lacked many little things which the Hotel-Dieu could not supply. Thus they went to Vincent de Paul to urge him to find a way to bring assistance to this great hospital.

The ever prudent Vincent hesitated to assume such a task. He had great respect for the administrators of the institution and for the more than fifty religious women who cared for the sick. He found himself in the very delicate position of trying to improve service in an already functioning institution over which he had no control. The Archbishop of Paris was asked to use his influence to persuade Vincent. In the meantime, Louise de Marillac was already at the hospital bringing whatever assistance she could to the sick. Vincent expressed fear for her health: "My God, Mademoiselle, how it grieves me to see you go so long without getting away for a rest because of the continual work you are doing at the Hotel-Dieu."

Much time and discussion were needed before the Ladies determined that the work should be continued and expanded. Finally Louise received the following directive from Vincent:

> You and your daughters are needed for the Hotel-Dieu. Four are considered necessary for the beginning. Please manage to find four good ones.

However, the "four good ones" were not good enough. They would remain only a few days since the Ladies felt that city girls would be better qualified to assist them than the rustic Daughters of Charity. Experience would soon prove them mistaken, so once again they asked Vincent to call upon the services of the girls trained by Louise.

Once the matter of personnel was settled, practical means for carrying out the service of the sick were developed. A room was rented near the Hotel-Dieu to store linen and to prepare food: bouillon, milk, white bread, biscuits, preserves and stewed fruits. Genevieve, Jacqueline, Germaine and Nicole worked tirelessly to prepare things tastefully for the sick. Neither the sisters nor the Ladies were afraid to risk their lives during times of epidemics. Isabelle and Marie fell ill. When one of the sisters died from a disease contracted at the hospital, Vincent wrote to Louise, "I hope that she died happy since she has given her life in the exercise of charity, for the love of God."

The spiritual service of the sick was added to corporal assistance. Abelly, the first biographer of Vincent, speaks of 760 persons "who had fallen away from the practice of their Faith who were converted" through contact with the sisters and the Ladies. A handbook was drawn up for those who visited the sick, containing the principal points of the instruction to be given to them. The following recommendation to the Ladies of Charity reveals Vincent's deep sensitivity to the poor. He reminds them:

> They should dress as simply as possible on the days they go to the Hotel-Dieu so that, if they cannot appear as poor among the poor, at least they will not add to the suffering of those who, upon seeing the extravagance and superfluities of the rich, become yet more troubled by their own lack of the basic necessities.

The example given by the sisters and the Ladies had another practical result. The Confraternities were no longer obliged to serve bouillon since the administration assumed this responsibility—a small thing today, no doubt, but it was a considerable gain at the time in the struggle for better service for the sick poor.

The work undertaken by the sisters at the Hotel-Dieu was a work of collaboration. Soon they would be called upon to take complete charge of hospitals around Paris and in the provinces. The sisters went to Angers, Le Mans, Nantes, Fontainebleau and Saint-Denis. Their efforts were not always crowned with success, yet Louise was able to inculcate in their hearts an esteem for their vocation, an awareness of "the great happiness they had of serving Our Lord in the person of the poor." Everywhere their love pushed them to quality service to which they brought the human dimension of concern for the person. At Saint-Denis, for example, we see the beginnings of hospital social work. Young girls are assisted in finding suitable work before being discharged.

War, both civil and foreign, would open up yet another field of action for Louise and her daughters. New cries of anguish touched the hearts of the founders as the sisters departed for the battlefields: Chalons, 1650; Estampes, 1652; Sedan, 1654; La Fere and Arras, 1656; Calais and Metz, 1658.

In the conference of August 4, 1658, to four sisters preparing to leave for Calais, Vincent said:

> You have been chosen to care for poor soldiers wounded in the service of the King . . . of the four sisters already sent there, one is dead and the others are very ill. Yet in spite of that, others have come forward to replace them and have said, "Sir, here I am, quite ready." As all of you have done, my Daughters. For there is not a single one of you who does not say that in her heart and who would not prove it by deeds, if she were needed . . . Then, Sisters, you should nurse those poor sick with great charity and gentleness so that they may see that you

are going to their assistance with a heart filled with compassion for them.

Since there were young women in the group destined for Calais who had recently entered the Company, Vincent reassured them: "Ah, my Daughters, don't be afraid; you will make a good novitiate." He then continued:

> I come to share in your joy and in Mademoiselle Le Gras' consolation for the choice which God has made of this little Company which He established Himself . . . It is quite evident that Our Lord formed it on the model of His own life. What did He come into this world to do, if not to save people? And what are you doing if not striving to save the lives of poor people?

It took a great spirit of daring to send simple young girls to the battlefield, but the "better service" of the poor urged them on. Her youthful timidity a thing of the past, Louise de Marillac daily renewed the courage of her daughters:

> Do not be afraid to undertake long journeys. Fear nothing in carrying out what God asks of you for His service and for that of the poor.

This desire to respond to whatever God was asking of them caused Louise and the sisters to turn toward yet another neglected group: young country girls. From the time of her earliest visits to the Confraternities of Charity, Mademoiselle Le Gras had been struck by their plight. With no opportunity for schooling, they were doomed to a miserable existence. Gobillon tells us that in an effort to remedy the situation, Louise gave pedagogical hints to the village school mistress, or, where there was none, she remained long enough to train someone for this role.

Her great flexibility in adapting methods to meet local conditions was her key to success. Moreover, she sought the education of the whole person. Religious instruction was not sterile recitation but a means for understanding life. As early as 1631, Vincent de Paul wrote to the pastor of Bergeres asking him to urge his people to send their children to school and citing the success of the work of Louise in education at Montmirail and Villepreux.

However, at this period Louise did not remain in one place for very long. In an effort to find young women capable of taking over the work after her departure, she sought those who desired to make God known and loved as well as to teach the basics of reading, writing and arithmetic. In 1632 Vincent wrote to Louise:

> I think that it is an excellent idea to have a school mistress at Villeneuve, but where are we going to find one? I can only suggest that you tell the mothers of your little pupils that you will send them one as soon as possible and that you will confer with them later concerning her board and housing.

Marguerite Naseau of Suresnes had led the way. As the years passed, other young women joined Louise. She sent them to teach the little country girls. At the same time, she urged them "to train some of them to teach in their absence. This they should do for the love of God and without any remuneration."

But the sisters themselves had first to be trained as teachers. Time was allowed by rule for study. Louise frequently undertook the task of teaching them to read and write "so that they could instruct poor little girls" wherever they were asked for. Schools were opened in Richelieu and Nanteuil. Generally, two sisters were sent together. Of one such pair Vincent wrote, "The two servants of the poor are accomplishing wonders—one with the sick, one in the instruction of little girls."

Later a sort of normal school was established at the motherhouse located in the parish of Saint-Laurent. Since the city schools were under the direction of the Canons of Notre Dame, Louise addressed her request to open a school in Paris to their superior. She wrote:

> I hope that God will be glorified by this work which would permit the poor to send their children to school without cost or interference from the rich.

Her request was granted with the following restriction:

> We grant you a license and the authorization to open a school in the area referred to as Saint-Lazare in the Saint-Denis district. It shall be for the instruction of *poor little girls only* and *no others.*

Louise was careful to stress this preference for poor children in the Rules of the Daughters of Charity. She wrote:

> The sisters shall know that all sorts of girls are not to be received into their school but only those who are poor. However, if Providence and obedience call them to a parish where there is no mistress for the instruction of the rich and their parents earnestly request them to receive them among their pupils, they shall do so with the approval of the pastor—but only on the condition that the poor always be preferred to the rich and that the rich do not look down on them.

For Louise and her first school mistress, the principal goal was to instruct these little girls in the truths of their Faith. To help them, Louise drew up a very simple catechism where the essentials to be learned were contained in a few words:

Q. Who created you and put you on earth?
A. God, so that we may love and serve Him and so that He may bring us to Heaven.

Q. How do you know God?
A. Through our Faith.

Q. To whom do we speak when we say the *Our Father?*
A. To God, whom we call our Father.

Q. Does God see our thoughts?
A. Yes.

Q. Where is He that He can see us?
A. He is everywhere.

Q. Does He see us when we offend Him?
A. Yes, He does.

Q. How should we speak to God as our Father?
A. With great love and the confidence that He will give us all we ask of Him, just as He has promised.

Q. What is the *Ave Maria?*
A. It was the greeting of the Angel when he came to ask the Blessed Virgin if she would become the mother of Jesus Christ, the Son of God. It is a devotion which is very pleasing to God.

Q. Who was the human father of Jesus Christ?
A. He does not have one.

Q. Who formed the body of Jesus in the womb of the Blessed Virgin?
A. The Holy Spirit.

Q. Was St. Joseph not her husband?
A. Yes, but he was given her as her guardian.

Louise de Marillac's role as an educator went well beyond the limits of the free school in the parish of Saint-Laurent. At Montreuil she was asked "to teach the girls a trade." In another area there was a request for a workroom where the pupils would make stockings and lace. She encouraged the sisters in the villages to gather the older girls together for an evening of "Gospel sharing." She advised the sisters who were traveling to take an interest in the girls they met in the inns where they were staying. In the country she urged them to be particularly mindful of the needs of the cowherds and the shepherdesses. In her directives to the sisters, Louise stressed the delicacy which must characterize their charity. She recommended that the Rule be strictly observed, but then she added the words, "if the service of the poor permits." Therefore, the sisters must "receive all these little girls who come to them to learn at whatever time they are free . . . placing those who are bashful or timid in a special place and welcoming all of them cordially, even when they come during meals." A formal exception to the Rule is made for "poor little girls who must beg for their bread or earn their own livings. They shall always prefer them to the rich and receive them whenever they come."

Total availability to poor young girls was the goal of the sisters engaged in education. However, they never lost sight of their ultimate aim: "You will teach these poor girls all you can, but you will always remember that the most important element in their instruction is the knowledge of God and of His love for them."

In the free school of Paris and in distant villages, Louise and her companions had found yet another way to provide "better service" for the poor.

As the years passed and the service of the poor expanded, still greater miseries befell the country. Once again Vincent de Paul and Louise de Marillac would heed the urgent cries of the needy, this time the victims of civil war which had broken out in France in 1650.

After the siege of Guise, Vincent sent two of his missionaries to bring supplies and money to the sick and dying soldiers. When Madame de Lamoignon offered him 800,000 pounds to build a house and church at Saint-Lazare, he thanked her but added, "This money would be better spent in assisting the poor of Picardy and Champagne." She granted his request.

The treaty of Westphalia of 1648 had not, as had been hoped, brought an end to all hostilities. Spain continued to occupy northern France. For twenty-five years armies from France, Spain, Germany and Lorraine ravaged the countryside, leaving behind them a trail of slaughter, pillage, and violence. In his *Misery at the Time of the Fronde and Saint Vincent de Paul,* de Feillet describes the horror of the period and the saint's efforts to alleviate it.

Vincent had already assisted the people of Lorraine who had experienced the same suffering prior to the Treaty of Westphalia. He now gave himself, without counting the cost, to relieving the misery in Picardy, Champagne and the Isle-de-France. For her part, Louise de Marillac was to find in the horror of civil war another area for "better service."

Money was the first necessity. Vincent mobilized the Ladies of Charity to whom he read the accounts of his missionaries who were serving the victims of war. But the Ladies alone could not furnish sufficient resources. It was decided to share the news of the most ravaged areas with all who would listen. Soon newsletters were being sent to the principal cities of France. They brought forth generous contributions which were carefully distributed. The Company of the Blessed Sacrament collaborated in this effort. Wisely, Vincent insisted that alms be limited to those who could not work. The others were to receive tools, seed and other necessities which would enable them to start life over again.

The donations were entrusted to the Priests of the Mission who left for the war area. In December 1650 there were seven priests and six brothers in the war relief effort. In 1651 their number increased to eighteen and there were still at least ten involved in the work in 1652. They were very quickly to discover that money alone was not sufficient. There were other great needs. Thus it was that Louise de Marillac's daughters were called to the care of the sick, orphans and the abandoned elderly, despite the dangers posed by plundering and rampaging armies. Never for a minute did they hesitate. Prudently, however, Vincent de Paul obtained a safe-conduct for them. The documents, dated February 14, 1651, advised all authorities, civil and military, to respect them. It read: "His Majesty forbids all warring parties to take anything from the Priests of the Mission or from persons employed with them or by them under pain of death."

At Rethel and Saint-Etienne, the sisters nursed the sick and wounded. Elsewhere they cared for orphans. The accounts of the period show that their number increased dramatically in a very short time. In 1650, there were thirty-five. In the next few years there would be 1,100—600 of whom were under seven years of age. Moreover, the Priests of the Mission would discover another 6,000 abandoned little ones in the villages to which they went to distribute alms. The sisters were aided in this gigantic task by the women of the region who made clothes from the material sent from Paris.

Once begun, the work would continue. From another account, dated December, 1655, we learn:

> The Sisters of Charity are housed in the Priory of Saint-Thibault-les-Bazoches. There they prepare food and remedies for the sick. The poor arrive with the tickets which we have given them to get their rations. If they are unable to walk, food is brought to them. The Daughters of Charity go wherever they can. They bleed the sick and give necessary remedies. There has been a visible improvement in their health.

The same report goes on to say that the sisters often found infants beside their dead mothers and that the sick they cared for numbered 1,200. It concludes with a plea for help: "We willingly give our lives for these poor unfortunates. Can you not give your money?" It was more than a plea. It was a reality which Louise de Marillac supported with all the strength of her being. She wrote to her companions, "We grieve for your suffering, but many of us are jealous of the service you are thus rendering to God."

Two sisters had been sent to Estampes in 1651. After the invasion by the forces of the Fronde, May 4, 1652, Louise sent others. They set up soup kitchens not only in the city but also in the surrounding villages. Thousands of the poor flocked to them. Orphans were sheltered and cared for. The work was exhausting for the missionaries and for the sisters. Many of them became ill. Sister Marie-Joseph would die in this service of the poor. She had already spent two years in Picardy and Champagne before arriving in Estampes. There she finally dropped from exhaustion. However, when she was informed that a poor woman needed to be bled, she tried to go to her. She died in the attempt. Vincent de Paul spoke of her to her companions as a "martyr of charity." Louise de Marillac encouraged them to emulate her zeal:

"Possess a heart as great as hers which finds nothing too difficult if performed for the love of God."

The Fronde was finally defeated, but the miseries of war continued. During the political struggles of 1652, soldiers pillaged and plundered the countryside. The population of entire villages fled to the capital where there were already 100,000 beggars. Famine became a permanent condition. Vincent de Paul described the situation:

> The misfortunes of the poor are so great that Mademoiselle Le Gras does not have enough sisters to assist the sick and the refugees in all the places that they are asked for. Many parishes have soup kitchens. Our sisters at Saint-Paul serve more than 8,000 poor people each day besides caring for the sixty to eighty sick for whom they are responsible.

At the motherhouse another 1,300 bashful poor were assisted, along with 800 refugees. In the outskirts of Paris death and destruction ran rampant.

To meet the situation, Vincent and Louise organized a "charitable warehouse" where they accepted gifts of money and goods. All the trade guilds of Paris gave what they could. The butchers gave meat, the tailors gave new and used clothing ... Everything was accepted. The sisters cleaned and repaired whatever was received. Packages were shipped by boat from the Isle Saint-Louis or transported by road to Villeneuve-Saint-Georges, Juvisy and Gonesse to be distributed at carefully selected centers. Medical teams composed of a doctor and sister nurses went about caring for the sick in what remained of their homes. 193 villages were saved as a result of this collective effort.

Throughout this endless conflict, Louise de Marillac continued to send her daughters to the battlefields. On September 16, 1658 she wrote, "I do not know if you have heard that Sister Francoise Manceaux and Sister Marguerite Menage died gallantly while serving the sick and wounded in Calais." Another sister was wounded at Chalons. However, as soon as she had recovered, she and three companions left for the battlefields of Sedan. They served in field hospitals in Sainte-Menehoult and La Fere. Other sisters went to Bernay and Angers to care for the plague-stricken. From Paris came words of encouragement. Vincent wrote:

> Believe that God will look after you wherever you go. Remain steadfast and never lose confidence in Divine Providence, even on the battlefield. Do not fear. No evil will befall you. Should one of you lose her life, know that it is a blessing for her since she will appear before God laden with merit, having given her life for charity.

Louise added, "Fear no evil, but bear whatever comes in submission to the divine pleasure." Truly Louise de Marillac and her daughters had found a way to provide "better service" to the victims of war.

In the work with the foundlings, Louise de Marillac had discovered misery in an institution which totally lacked the means to respond to the goals for which it had been created. She took it upon herself to completely reorganize the work and to place the children in another, more appropriate setting. At the Hotel-Dieu, she and her sisters had worked, along with the Ladies of Charity, as volunteers. They had collaborated with the administrators and staff of an institution which, while good in itself, had failed to evolve with the times.

The work with the aged would be a completely new creation for her. According to Abelly, the funds were to come from "a rich merchant of Paris who had offered Vincent a large sum of money." Brother Ducournau, Vincent's secre-

tary, claims that this money was intended for the houses of
the Congregation of the Mission, but that, in his usual style,
Vincent de Paul placed the needs of the poor before those
of his company. Thus he asked his benefactor if he could
employ the entire sum to shelter and care for elderly ar-
tisans who, at a period when there were no pensions or
social security, had been reduced by age and infirmity to
destitution. According to a contract drawn up September
28, 1647, two houses were acquired in the Saint-Laurent
district "to shelter, feed and clothe forty poor of both
sexes."

Louise de Marillac assumed full responsibility for
organizing the work, as well as for providing the sisters to
serve the aged. She gave herself wholeheartedly to her task,
reflecting on it before God and applying to it all the
resources of a mind and heart capable of discerning the
needs of the future as well as those of the present. She
would say:

> The greater the work the more important it is to
> establish it on a solid foundation. Thus it will not
> only be more perfect; it will also be more lasting.

Since the number of places was limited, the selection
process was a difficult one. They did not want to accept
professional beggars, but rather elderly workers of good
reputation. They sought to create a pleasant productive at-
mosphere in the house. God would occupy the first place
and Vincent would frequently come to speak to the residents of Him in his simple, direct way. The texts which we
still possess show the admiration and respect which he had
for each of them.

For her part, Louise de Marillac understood that the fear
of being a burden to others was the greatest suffering of old
age. In the program of the house she wrote, "For the
spiritual and temporal effectiveness of the house, it is es-

sential that no one should feel useless, especially in the beginning."

The organization of the work incorporated concepts which foreshadowed present-day occupational therapy. Craftsmen were asked to set up workrooms where the residents could be employed at tasks which were in keeping with their diminishing strength, but which would also be interesting and profitable. They were thus able to work at their former trades as weavers, shoemakers, buttonmakers, lacemakers and dressmakers. They were even commissioned to do some work for shops in Paris. Concerning all this, Louise commented, "If some profit is made on the work, it is so that the house can be expanded and more elderly persons cared for."

But the residents themselves were also interested in turning a profit from their endeavors, since each one received a quarter of the money earned from his work. Since everything was provided for them except wine, this gave them a little personal spending money. The measure proved to be a wise one, for more often than not the earnings of the men went, in whole or in part, to "good cheer." In general the women were a bit more cautious in spending the fruits of their labors.

The original intent of the contract of October 29, 1653, which was to prevent the spread of mendicity, "the mother of all vices," by providing for the care of elderly workers in the Hospice of the Holy Name of Jesus, was admirably fulfilled—thanks to the creative genius of Louise de Marillac. News of her success soon reached the Ladies of Charity, who wanted to extend the work to all the beggars of Paris. The Company of the Blessed Sacrament had one of its members involved exclusively in this work. However, the approach was entirely different. Whereas the Ladies of Charity worked publicly, the members of the Company of the Blessed Sacrament hid their charitable actions. This precluded their participation in any established work.

Moreover, the Ladies seemed to believe that charity was more properly the work of women. In one of their documents we read:

> If a work is political, it would appear that it should be undertaken by men. However, if it is considered a work of charity, women may accomplish it in the same way that they have accomplished other great and difficult exercises of charity which God, in His goodness, has blessed.

The Ladies met with Vincent de Paul and urged him to begin immediately. As usual, he delayed making a decision. However, he did initiate some action. He obtained the land of the Salpetriere from the Queen. The first beggars were to be accepted on a trial basis. Vincent told the Ladies:

> Let us first experiment. Let us accept only 100 to 200 poor persons, and then only those who want to come. No one should be forced. If those who arrive first are well treated and happy, they will attract others. Thus, little by little, the number will grow in keeping with the resources which Divine Providence will furnish. Nothing is lost by acting in this way. On the contrary, precipitation and constraint are a hindrance to the design of God.

Construction was begun on the land of the Salpetriere. However, opposition to the original plan soon appeared. Its scope was considered too narrow. The undesirable poor had to be removed from the streets. In 1656 a royal edict outlawed begging. Of the 40,000 poor who solicited alms from the citizens of Paris, only 4,000 - 5,000 were willing to enter the general hospital or its annexes. The Regent decreed that the Congregation of the Mission should provide for the spiritual welfare of the inmates. Unwilling to collaborate in this effort to deprive the poor of their liberty Vincent de Paul refused. Louise de Marillac, however, sent two sisters to help care for the women internees.

Thus it was that Louise and her companions found at the Hospice of the Holy Name of Jesus and the Salpetriere yet another way to render "better service" to the poor.

If the lot of beggars in seventeenth-century Paris was lamentable, the fate of the mentally ill was tragic. Their suffering was not unknown to Vincent de Paul. When he took possession of the Priory of Saint-Lazare, he assumed the care of a number of sick and mentally ill persons. He would grow to love them so dearly that he said that it would be these suffering souls, ill in body or in mind, whom he would miss the most were he ever called upon to leave Saint-Lazare.

As always, his charity would not be limited to his own house. The Office for the Poor which had been established in the sixteenth century to counteract mendicity, was at this period in a large hospital which housed 400 poor, elderly, ill and insane men and women. Vincent himself described the conditions there:

> At the Petites Maisons there are all sorts of insane and mentally disturbed persons crowded together. There is continual quarreling. It is truly incredible. There is such hostility that not even two of them can remain together for long. They have to be separated and each one crouches and broods in his corner.

The full extent of the misery of these poor people became even more apparent to Vincent in 1639 when he preached a mission to them. He prepared a small booklet for their use which included the main truths of the Catholic Faith and a selection of prayers. After the mission, the work of catechizing these poor unfortunates was continued by the priests of the Tuesday Conference.

Naturally, Vincent frequently discussed the work with his friend and collaborator, Louise de Marillac. Together they prepared to send sisters to the Petites Maisons to care for the mentally ill and the sick women patients. One of the most outstanding of the early Daughters of Charity was selected to begin this work. In honor of the occasion, Louise asked Vincent "to speak to the sisters on the good that could be accomplished in such a place." On December 18, 1655, the sisters assembled to hear him. Deriving his inspiration from the Gospel and from the life of Jesus Christ, Vincent reminded them:

> I would have you know, Sisters, that Our Lord willed to experience in His own Person all imaginable miseries. The scriptural expression is that it was His will to be a scandal to the Jews and a folly to the Gentiles in order to show you that you can serve Him in all these poor afflicted persons. And hence it is that He willed to enter on this state, that He might sanctify it as He did all others. You must know that He is present in those poor folk devoid of intelligence as He is in everybody else. It is with this in mind that you should render them service, and when you go amongst them you should rejoice and say to yourself, "I am going to those poor folk to honor in their persons the Person of Our Lord; I am going to see in them the Incarnate Wisdom of God who willed to pass for such, though He was not so in reality."

Vincent frequently came to visit the sisters at their work. Once again their tasks were humble: laundry, cooking, the infirmary—but everything was carried out in a spirit of love which won all hearts.

At this period there were about seventy mentally ill patients. However, the infirmary had only eighteen beds: four for the men and fourteen for the women. Quickly, the number seeking care grew. Places had to be reserved far in advance. At one time even Vincent himself was unable to place a patient. He wrote, "It is impossible to have this poor disturbed man admitted to the Petites Maisons since there is never an empty bed. These are reserved long before they are available."

Abelly testifies that "the administrators paid tribute to the Daughters of Charity for having rectified a number of disorders which offended God, damaged the reputation of the house, and caused additional suffering for the patients." Here as elsewhere, the sisters were living the Rule given to them by Vincent and Louise:

> . . . to serve the poor with joy, courage, constancy and love . . . to be very careful of the goods of the poor and the interests of the house . . . to be faithful to prayer, even while coming and going, if time does not permit you to make your meditation in the chapel.

In a word, they were to bring the loving hand of Christ into the dehumanized world of mental illness.

This is not to say that all went well. The history of the work speaks of a serious altercation between the chaplain and the sister in charge. The administrators became aware of the situation and tried to mediate. At this point, Louise intervened and threatened to withdraw the sisters "should any dishonor befall the chaplain, whom we are obliged to respect." The sisters also suffered ill treatment from the patients. They accepted everything without resentment while continuing to serve the poor in the spirit of Sister Nicole, whose work became legendary. One account relates:

> They admitted a poor mental patient who had an

infected, decaying leg, filled with vermin. He had had the wound for a very long time. He had been a boarder in a private home for three years during which time he had been treated by surgeons who had applied every imaginable remedy but without any success. He was judged incurable. When he was admitted, the house surgeon saw him. He soon abandoned treatment as did the male nurses who were repulsed by his infection. At this point, Sister Nicole took charge of him. She cared for him with such gentleness and confidence in God that she cured him in a very short time simply by using ordinary remedies.

Once again, yet another group of poor were "better served." However, the borders of France would soon prove too narrow for the charitable zeal of Vincent and Louise. In 1653 their Daughters of Charity would leave for Poland.

Among the 120 Ladies of Charity of the Hotel-Dieu of Paris, one stood out because of her remarkable beauty and her extraordinary goodness toward the poor to whom she had been introduced by Vincent de Paul. She was Louise-Marie de Gonzague, who became Queen of Poland in 1645. Even after the death of her husband, Wladislas IV, she retained her position by her marriage to the dead king's brother, John Casimir. In her new homeland she never forgot Vincent de Paul, whom she venerated, calling him "the angel of the Lord who bears on his lips the ardent fires of divine love which burn in his heart."

While still in France, the young queen had seen the work of the first Priests of the Mission. She knew Louise de Marillac and she loved the humble Daughters of Charity who devoted themselves to the poor alongside the Ladies of Charity of the Hotel-Dieu. When misery befell her kingdom, she requested the assistance of these sisters trained by Louise. They would join the Priests of the Mission, who had arrived in Poland shortly after her ascension to the throne. In a Conference dated July 14, 1651, Vincent spoke to the sisters of the Queen's request:

> This should give you great courage, my dear Daughters, to cherish the dispositions which God has given you, because by the grace of God, I do not know that it has ever happened that any single one of you ever refused to go where she was sent. No, I don't know of one . . . I know, my Daughters, that people more than 600 leagues away are asking for you; I have had letters from them. Yes, people more than 600 leagues away are thinking of you; and if there are queens who are asking for you, I also know of others beyond the seas who are asking for you.

It would be two years before three sisters would finally depart on the long, wearying journey through the Baltics and across Germany to join the Queen in Lowicz. After a period of adaptation during which the sisters became acclimated to their new environment, the Queen decided to send two of them to Krakow to serve the poor, while the third one was to remain with her. However, the sister in question, Marguerite Moreau, protested:

> Ah, Madame, what are you asking? We are only three to serve the poor. There are many persons in the kingdom more capable than we are to serve your Majesty. Permit us, Madame, to do what God asks of us here and what we do elsewhere. "What, you do not want to serve me," said the Queen. Pardon me, Madame, but it is God who has called us to serve the poor.

Sister Marguerite made her point. The formation given

by Louise was bearing fruit.

This foundation, just like so many other new works, had a difficult beginning, caused primarily by an official appointed by the Queen to supervise the sisters. Not satisfied with overseeing their work, the supervisor tried to control their lives. The matter was finally settled, and the Queen requested additional sisters. In 1655 they left for Rouen on the first leg of their journey to join their three companions. However, the advance of Russian troops on Warsaw obliged them to postpone the remainder of their trip.

In the meantime, the first sisters continued to serve the poor in Warsaw and later in Silicia. The Poles regained possession of their capital in 1657 after a long siege during which the sisters nursed the wounded. They had previously opened a school into which they now accepted children orphaned by the war.

In 1660 another group of sisters was chosen for Poland. This was one of the last joys of Vincent de Paul. Although Louise did not live to see them depart, she was present in the minds and hearts of her daughters, since it was she who had formed in them that spirit of charity and abnegation which would cause Vincent de Paul to exclaim, ten days before his death, "Blessed be God who has thus disposed the hearts of His daughters. They are asked to go to Poland, and they are ready!"

However, it was not only to Poland that they were ready to go. On September 29, 1655, the young Company had gathered around Vincent and Louise while he spoke to them of the joy to be found in the service of the poor:

> What a consolation to feel certain that one is pleasing God, that one is doing what God wills and giving joy to God! What a consolation for a father to see his children doing his will! This holds true of God, Sisters. He is pleased to see persons who will only what He wills . . . Give thanks to God that you

are associated with His Son in giving Him joy and pleasure.

... You should be ready to go anywhere, because you are being asked for on all sides ...

In Madagascar, our gentlemen beg us to send them Daughters of Charity to help them win souls. Fathers Mousnier and Bourdaise tell me that they believe that this is an essential step in leading the local population to the Faith. They would like a hospital for the sick and a school for the education of girls. They are also asking that we send some of the foundlings who know how to work so that they can teach others. And that is why you should be prepared to go there. It is a journey of 4,500 leagues and takes six months. Sisters, I am telling you this that you may see God's designs on you. So dispose yourselves, my Daughters, and give your-selves to Our Lord to go wherever it may please Him.

Are you resolved to go everywhere without ex-ception?

"Yes, Father," they replied.

But are you really so disposed? If so, tell me.

All the sisters stood up and again declared that they were.

Two centuries would pass before the dream of having sisters in Madagascar would become a reality, but the seed had been planted. It would eventually bear fruit.

In France and beyond her borders, wherever the misery of the times would call them, Louise de Marillac and her daughters found a way to provide "better service" for the poor.

Chapter VII

NEW BEGINNINGS

Multifaceted action can never be the work of a single person. As the years passed, the scope of the charitable activity to which Louise de Marillac devoted her life widened as her love for Jesus Christ, whom she served in the poor, deepened. Her relationship with Vincent de Paul, whom she met in about the year 1623, was to prove decisive in this regard. Prior to her contact with him, she had helped her neighbor in a limited way. Under his guidance, her horizon expanded. More and more she penetrated the mystery of the identification of Christ with the poor: "Whatsoever you do to the least of mine, that you do unto me." Soon she would no longer be content simply to bring a few delicacies to a poor person, to care for a sick neighbor, to find shelter for a needy individual or to procure employment for a young girl. Although these efforts would continue for a number of years, she would, at the same time, become President of one of the first Confraternities of Charity in Paris, that of her own parish, Saint-Nicolas-du-Chardonnet. Thus she would renew her contacts with the noble families of the fashionable Marais district, and "together" they would serve the poor, including the galley slaves.

After a period of discernment during which they sought to discover the will of God in her regard, Vincent de Paul sent Louise, in 1629, to visit the Confraternities of Charity which he and his priests had established in the provinces and in the outskirts of Paris. In collaboration with the Ladies of Charity throughout France, she made her apprenticeship in the corporal and spiritual service of the sick and the needy.

The discreet but firm influence of Vincent de Paul continued to guide Louise toward the total dedication of her life to the service of the poor. Their collaboration grew ever closer. From the earliest days of their relationship, Vincent had kept her informed of his apostolic endeavors. Now, however, he elicited her active participation and sought her advice: "What do you think, Mademoiselle?"

New projects would follow one another in rapid succession as the whole gamut of human miseries became apparent to their zealous hearts. Success and failure marked these endeavors. But there were many more successes than failures since everything was carefully and prayerfully considered before being undertaken. Vincent was wont to say, "Our Lord wants us to serve Him prudently. The opposite is called excessive zeal." If the maxim was Vincent's, its application was frequently reiterated by Louise. On one occasion she wrote:

> Since I wanted to reflect on this work before God, I realized that I must examine every aspect of it: its beginning, its continuation and its possible conclusion. The greater the work, the more important it is to establish it on a solid foundation. Thus it will be more perfect and more lasting.

If Vincent constantly recommended that they avoid "anticipating Divine Providence," neither of them would ever abandon a work, whatever the difficulties they might encounter, once it had been determined after prayerful discernment that God had willed it.

Louise de Marillac has frequently been portrayed as a simple disciple following the directives of a venerated master. Nothing could be further from the truth. Vincent de Paul had too much respect for the person of Louise not to allow her to give the full measure of her extraordinary talents in the service of God and of the poor. Although he was always there to support her in times of crisis, he usually urged her to use her own initiative. "Do what you judge best," was his frequent reply to the questions she addressed to him. It was rather in mutual support for one another that they advanced to combat human misery wherever they found it. This union makes it vain to try to establish which of them had the greater part in their numerous charitable undertakings. What they did, they did in respectful collaboration—except, of course, for the works dealing with the reform of the clergy, which must be attributed entirely to Vincent. For the rest, they worked together for nearly forty years.

Vincent de Paul and Louise de Marillac were not alone in the great charitable and mystical renewal which marked the first half of the seventeenth century. The Company of the Blessed Sacrament worked unnoticed for the same end and frequently in collaboration with Vincent and Louise. Several congregations of religious women were founded in France to assist the poor. Among them were the Daughters of Providence who cared for girls and women in moral danger, and the Daughters of the Cross who received great support from Vincent in their charitable endeavors. Far from seeking exclusivity in their undertakings, Vincent and Louise contributed what they could to alleviate human misery by initiating, supporting or collaborating in charitable enterprises. Often their collaboration went unnoticed, but, according to Louise, "Provided God is glorified, that suffices." This total lack of self-interest explains, in large measure, their influence and their success.

The Ladies of Charity proved to be an indispensable support in this vast network of charity. As Louise had done before them, Madame Goussault and Mademoiselle

Pollalion, Treasurer of the Ladies of the Hotel-Dieu, would visit the Confraternities of Charity in the provinces. The Duchess of Aiguillon, a niece of Richelieu, made an annual contribution of 200 gold pieces to help feed the sick who were cared for by the sisters. The Princess of Conde and Mademoiselle Violle played important roles in the care of the foundlings. Great was the joy of Vincent when the Ladies voted to extend this work to all the foundlings of the capital. At the request of various members, the Ladies also opened several hospitals and houses of charity for which Louise chose the personnel from among the Daughters of Charity. They even extended their work as far as Poland in the person of Queen Louise-Marie de Gonzague.

This is not to say that this collaboration was without difficulty. As in any organization, there were some who wanted to take over everything, others who had to be pushed to fulfill the conditions of a contract, and many more who, after a first burst of enthusiasm, gave way to indifference, putting the whole undertaking in jeopardy. A telling instance of this is recorded in Vincent's fervent appeal to the Ladies concerning the fate of the foundlings. He had been pushed into confronting them by Louise's anguished plea in behalf of the unpaid foster mothers who were forced to return the infants to the sisters because they were too poor and exhausted to continue providing milk. With rare eloquence, Vincent challenged them:

> Charity and compassion moved you to adopt these poor creatures as your children. Are you now also going to abandon them? Their lives and their deaths are in your hands.

Collaboration in this great work and in many others continued. In a meeting held a short time later, Vincent said of the foundlings, "They are housed with the Daughters of Charity, and Mademoiselle Le Gras is providing for them."

Vincent and the Ladies of Charity lent their support, but in all her charitable endeavors, the closest collaborators of Louise de Marillac would be the Daughters of Charity.

By 1645, when the little group first sought recognition by the Church, they had been together for twelve years, leading a common fraternal life in which they were "totally given to God for the service of the poor." The request for approbation, addressed to Jean Francois de Gondi, Archbishop of Paris, gives a clear picture of their evolution. Louise had carefully weighed every word in this document signed by Vincent de Paul, and her humility would have caused her to eliminate her own role in what had occurred. Nevertheless, the simple truth prevailed. It reads in part:

> After the establishment of the Confraternities of Charity in several villages, some charitable women of Paris were so touched by what had been accomplished that they urged their pastors to establish similar groups in their parishes. This was done and God blessed their work.
>
> However, since the members of these Confraternities were, for the most part, noblewomen, their social condition and obligations did not permit them to carry out the more humble and disagreeable tasks such as carrying a soup pot through the city, bathing the sick, binding up their wounds, staying up with those who were alone, preparing their bodies for burial . . . Thus to assist them they took on some good country girls to whom God had given the desire to serve the poor after they had been trained by a virtuous widow named Mademoiselle Le Gras. To provide girls for the Confraternities, the aforesaid Mademoiselle Le Gras trained others in her home. Ordinarily, she had more than thirty young women working with

her whom she employed to teach poor little girls; to visit the sick of the parish, bringing food and medicine to them; or to respond to the needs of the poor who came to them for help.

The vast network of charity was spreading, but Vincent de Paul and Louise de Marillac both knew that for it to endure, something more was needed. Their charitable activity required solid roots, since, as the request for recognition by the Church points out, "works for the service of God generally end with those who have initiated them unless there is a *spiritual bond among those engaged in them.*" This "spiritual bond" was to be the vow made to God to serve the poor together in the Company of the Daughters of Charity. It is now time to examine more closely the nature of this consecration.

Chapter VIII

SOURCE AND MODEL
OF ALL CHARITY

The root of action for the Daughters of Charity, as for their founders, was to be the contemplation of Christ in the person of the poor with whom He is identified. Bremond's assessment of Vincent de Paul, found in his *Literary History of Religious Thought,* is equally applicable to Louise de Marillac. He wrote:

> It is not the poor who led him to God but rather
> God who led him to the poor. The greatest of our
> men of action was, first of all, a mystic.

Both Vincent and Louise were children of an era during which mysticism flourished. Close bonds united Vincent de Paul to Berulle and Olier, while Louise de Marillac maintained ties with her uncle Michel, the Carmelites and the Visitandines. Berulle wrote, "The whole design of the love of God on the world is summed up in the mystery of the Incarnation." Vincent and Louise shared this view, but they did not limit it to an intellectual contemplation of a mystery. Rather, they contemplated the Incarnate Word where He was hidden upon earth: in the person of the poor. Vincent would say, "The poor are Jesus Christ."

For the founders of the Daughters of Charity, not only did the Son of God, in becoming Man, choose to be poor and lowly, but He willed to be identified with the poor. In the Gospel He tells us, "Whatsoever you do for the least of mine, that you do unto me." This is so true that man's final judgment will depend on his treatment of the poor. To be convinced of this, it suffices to open the Gospel and to re-read Saint Matthew's account of the Last Judgment. Christ, the just Judge, says:

> Come, you whom my Father has blessed, take for your heritage the kingdom prepared for you since the foundation of the world. For I was hungry and you gave me food; I was thirsty and you gave me drink; I was a stranger and you made me welcome, naked and you clothed me, sick, and you visited me, in prison, and you came to see me . . . I tell you solemnly, in so far as you did this to one of the least of these brothers of mine, you did it to me.

Louise de Marillac daily lived these words of Christ as she responded to a call which became increasingly urgent, a call which Vincent de Paul helped her to discern and later translate into concrete reality.

As early as the first years of her widowhood, she foresaw the place that the "service of the neighbor" would occupy in her life. This is reflected in her retreat notes of this period during which she was seeking to discover God's will for her. The essential of her quest is found in a prayer which dates from this era:

> Free of every bond, to follow Jesus Christ, and to serve my neighbor with humility and gentleness.

In 1627 Vincent asked her to make shirts for the Confraternity of Charity of Gentilly. When she wrote to him to tell him that they were ready, she said, "If the members of Jesus need them, and you wish me to provide them, I shall gladly do so." The expression "members of Jesus" is frequently used by Louise. It bears the mark of the preciosity in language of the period in which she lived, but it contains a profound theological truth, that of the Mystical Body of Christ so dear to Saint Paul:

> All baptized in Christ, you have all clothed yourselves in Christ, and there are no more distinctions between Jew and Greek, slave and free, male and female, but all of you are one in Christ Jesus.

A few years later, when she was visiting the Confraternities of Charity, Louise often had occasion to remind the Ladies of this presence of God in the poor. While commenting on their Rule, she would reflect with them on the words which expressed the reason for their existence: "to honor Our Lord Jesus Christ in the person of His poor members." With even greater insistence would she recall this same truth to the Daughters of Charity as their "Little Company" was coming into being. The first article of their Rule centers their vocation on the call of God to contemplate, love and serve Him in the poor, since His Son, in becoming Man, willed to be identified with them. It reads:

> The principal end for which God has called and assembled the Daughters of Charity is to honor Our Lord Jesus Christ as the source and model of all charity, serving Him corporally and spiritually in the person of the poor, whether sick, children, prisoners or others who, through shame, dare not make known their wants.

This obligation to look upon the poor with the "eyes of faith" characterizes the spirit of the Daughters of Charity. Vincent de Paul and Louise de Marillac constantly sought to deepen this conviction. On August 29, 1648, Mademoiselle Le Gras wrote:

Let us have continually before our eyes our model which is the exemplary life of Jesus Christ whom we are called to imitate, not only as Christians, but also as women chosen by God to serve Him in the person of the poor.

Whether it be in spiritual conferences to the community, or correspondence, or the various texts of the early Rule drawn up by Vincent and Louise, the recurring theme was always the verse from Saint Paul which would become the motto of the Company: "The charity of Christ urges us."

The root of action is the contemplation of Christ in the poor. However, this contemplation which would permit them to "see" Christ in those whom they were called upon to serve had to be nourished by a life of prayer. Thus it was that the founders insisted that the sisters be faithful to prayer, every day, for at least one hour.

In 1633 these "good country girls" had banded together "to give themselves totally to God for the service of the poor." First as assistants to the Ladies of Charity, later as an independent Company recognized by the Church in France, they continued their lives of consecration. Where but in prayer would they draw the strength required to love God and their neighbor in this way? Patiently, Louise de Marillac led them to this union with God. Vincent continued to encourage them to persevere in their efforts. In his conferences to them, which have become the charter of the Company, he blends lofty thoughts with simple, practical advice, for it must be remembered that the greater number of these first Daughters of Charity were illiterate, as were the vast majority of women in the seventeenth century. So that they would not become discouraged by their limitations, Vincent suggested the use of pictures:

Make use of good-size pictures of the principal mysteries of the life and passion of Our Lord Jesus

Christ. Can one not make an excellent meditation by dwelling on the passion and death of our Savior?

During the Conferences of Vincent de Paul, the sisters took turns speaking. The quiet eloquence of Louise de Marillac blended with more simple but no less profound remarks of the other sisters. The Conference of May 31, 1648, on prayer, illustrates this procedure and at the same time reveals something of the prayer life of the early community. When called upon to speak, Mademoiselle Le Gras said:

> When we pray, we speak to God . . . This coming and indwelling of God in us is marked by a fullness of gifts and graces. I desired to give full consent to their reception . . . so that I may participate in the fullness the Apostles seem to have had, seeing that their understanding was enlightened and replenished with the knowledge necessary for their vocation, their memory quite refreshed concerning the words and actions of the Son of God, their will burning with His love and the love of their neighbor; and the plenitude of the Holy Spirit, strongly operating in them, taught them to speak of and to teach efficaciously the greatness and love of God. I greatly desired to glorify God in His wonderful works, to abandon myself to Him, so that in and by me He might work His most holy will . . .

One of the other sisters shared her thoughts:

> It is in prayer that we learn the will of God, we grow perfect, we acquire strength to resist temptations, and we strengthen ourselves in our vocation;

lastly, in prayer our soul has the happiness of speaking heart to heart with God. On the contrary, when we do not pray, we are weak, and we do not experience the presence of God during the day.

Finally, Vincent himself recalled the recommendations given by Christ, His promises and the example He left His followers. He then went on to speak of mental prayer:

> Prayer, my Daughters, is an elevation of the mind to God by which the soul detaches itself, as it were, from itself, so as to seek God in Himself. It is a conversation of the soul with God, an intercourse of the spirit in which God interiorly teaches it what it should know and do, in which the soul says to God what He Himself teaches it to ask for.
>   . . . The soul sees itself in God and conforms itself to Him in all things.
>   . . . It is in prayer that He enlightens her understanding with truths that are incomprehensible to those who do not pray . . . that He inflames wills . . . and takes possession of hearts and souls.

Elsewhere in his Conferences, Vincent de Paul insists on the importance of prayer in the life of a Daughter of Charity. On October 13, 1658, he said, "Prayer is the soul of our souls; what the soul is to the body, prayer is to the soul." In the Conference of May 31, 1648, he warned them, ". . . a Daughter of Charity cannot persevere if she does not pray. It is impossible . . . She may continue for some little time, but at length the world will carry her off. She will find her mode of life too hard." Over and over again, he urged them to "pray always." But he understood their difficulties and constantly encouraged them:

> Pray to God when you are troubled . . . Don't be

78

discouraged if you don't know how to read . . . God loves the poor and the lowly . . . who are often wiser in prayer than the learned . . . Our Lord Himself will be your teacher.

He was certain that, if they were faithful to prayer, God would reward their efforts. He told them, "O my Daughters, if you make your prayer well, what will you not then receive from God? As David has said, you will discover the greatness of the Lord."

However, Vincent de Paul was careful that the poor were not lost sight of in the prayer and daily activity of the Daughters of Charity. From the very beginning, he avoided creating a dichotomy between prayer and service by always stressing the unity of their lives. The love of God drawn in prayer was to be transformed into the love of the neighbor by means of concrete, practical resolutions. In the Conference of August 2, 1640, he gave them an example: "Your resolutions should be something like this: I will go and serve the poor; I will try to go to them with a modestly gay demeanor so as to console and edify them; I will speak to them as if they were my lords. There are some persons who seldom speak to me; I will bear with them . . ." On several occasions, Vincent repeated his famous adage of "leaving God for God." On October 13, 1658, he explained:

If you have to leave prayer to care for a sick person, do so. You will leave God in prayer and you will find Him in the person of the sick. To serve the sick is to make one's prayer.

The theme of prayer is frequently repeated in the Conferences, often at the request of Louise de Marillac. This is yet another example of the cooperative effort of two saints burning with the love of God and of His beloved poor. This love was to be strengthened and maintained by prayer and also by means of the sacraments, where the very life of God is communicated to His creatures.

Vincent and Louise urged the sisters to live a full sacramental life which would, in turn, bear fruit for the service of the poor. On January 22, 1646, Vincent gave a Conference on this subject which was recorded in Louise de Marillac's own handwriting. Early in this Conference she stated, "The benefit that accrues to us from a good Communion is that it makes us one with God." She then continued, "I thought it would be well to stir up in myself an ardent desire for Holy Communion, to act in such a way that the desire should always be like a new desire . . . and to have no other end in view than that of union with Our Lord."

Moved by her remarks, Vincent exclaimed:

> What! A poor Daughter of Charity, who before her Communion is merely what she is, who is not worth very much, now becomes one with God! Ah, my Daughters, who would be willing to neglect such a boon? Oh, what a grace! What do you think it is . . . but a pledge of eternity? Could we comprehend anything grander? . . . a poor, wretched creature is united with God; Oh, may He be forever blessed!

In his usual manner, Vincent then passed from the abstract to the concrete:

> . . . blessed are those souls who do all in their power to keep themselves in a state of being always able to make a good Holy Communion. These souls are always so tenderly cherished by God; never, never are they separated from His holy presence. But one of the reasons . . . which I regard as most important as far as your vocation is con-

cerned, is that you are destined by God to prepare
souls to die well. Do you think that God merely ex-
pects you to bring His poor a morsel of bread . . .
Oh, no . . . they are in need of heavenly manna . . .
and where will you find it, so that you can com-
municate it to them? In Holy Communion . . . let us
draw near to this fire to be first of all enkindled
ourselves, and then, by our charity and good example, to draw others to it.

On August 18, 1647, Vincent de Paul once again devoted
an entire Conference to the reception of Holy Communion.
During it a sister remarked that "when a person had
received Holy Communion well, she did everything well."
To which Vincent replied, "This is true, since she bears
God in her heart . . . she does nothing save with a view to
and for the love of God . . . Her heart is the tabernacle of
God—yes, the tabernacle of God. The Daughter of Charity
should always be that; she should always be in God and
God in her."

To the comment of another sister that after a good Communion a person would be "more gentle and charitable
toward the sick," Vincent responded:

> . . . what will a person not do who has God
within her, who is filled with God? She will not be
acting of herself, she will be doing the actions of
Jesus Christ; she will tend the sick with the charity
of Jesus Christ; she will have the gentleness of
Jesus Christ in her life and in her conversations;
she will have the patience of Jesus Christ in time of
trial . . . The Father will see His Son in such a person. What a grace . . . to be certain that we are
watched over by God, considered by God, loved by
God! And so when you see a Sister of Charity tend-
ing the sick gently, lovingly and attentively, you

may boldly say, "That sister made a good Communion."

Returning to the thoughts of Louise de Marillac on the union with Jesus Christ which is an effect of Holy Communion, Vincent added:

> Now, my Daughters, Jesus Christ is a friend and a bridegroom to souls who have given themselves to Him. He is more really a spouse than all the spouses of the world, and in an utterly different manner, because He is all heavenly and all divine. He is a friend more than all friends in the world, because He gave His blood and His life for each single soul.

Thus it was that the spiritual life of these simple country girls was rooted in the pure love of God. However, since community life was a school of perfection rather than perfection itself, there were weaknesses and failings. The sisters were encouraged to seek the pardon of Jesus Christ in the Sacrament of Penance. Like other "good Christians," they were urged to have frequent recourse to it. Once again the spiritual life was linked to the service of the poor. In a Conference of March 5, 1651, which spoke of preparation for the reception of the Sacrament of Penance, a sister remarked:

> We cannot teach the poor or school children to prepare well for confession if we do not do so ourselves.

This ever-expanding love of God and of the poor led the Daughters of Charity to give themselves more completely to God by vow. Very early in her life, Louise de Marillac had dedicated her entire being to the Lord of Charity. To her

vow of widowhood of 1623 she had added a vow to con-
secrate herself to the formation of the servants of the poor.
In 1624, at the time of her "Pentecost experience" in the
church of Saint-Nicolas-des-Champs, she had foreseen that
"the time would come when [she] could make vows of
poverty, chastity and obedience and that this would be done
while living with others, some of whom would do the
same."

At this period, Louise admitted that she did not see how
this would be possible. In her account of the event, she
tells us:

> I understood further that this would occur at a
> place devoted to assisting the neighbor, but I could
> not imagine how it would come about, for such a
> thing would require much coming and going.

"Coming and going" describes well the daily life of
Louise de Marillac and of the first village girls whom she
formed in the practice of poverty, chastity and obedience
for the "better service" of the poor. However, the question
of a commitment of a formal nature to God and to the in-
cipient community remained unresolved. Vincent and
Louise discussed the matter at great length. He was well
aware of the canonical difficulties in the way of such a step.
He had completed a licenciate in Canon Law in 1623 at the
University of Paris. Moreover, as Superior of the Visitation, he had seen with his own eyes how these religious
women, called to visit the sick, had been obliged to return to
a cloistered life. He feared that the same thing would hap-
pen to the Daughters of Charity since, at that period, the
Church did not recognize an active religious life for
women. Yet he saw this as the only way to insure the effective service of the poor. In a Conference on July 14, 1651,
he stated:

And how would those services be rendered to the poor, which, by the mercy of God, you do render them, if you could not leave a place? Who would go to those poor convicts? Who would nurse the sick in the villages? Who would visit those living in rented rooms or attics without any help or assistance?

Prudently, the founders waited. However, as early as July 19, 1640, Vincent had spoken to the sisters of the vows pronounced by Monks Hospitallers of Italy who committed themselves "to serve our lords, the poor." He then added, "Observe, my Daughters, how pleasing it is to our good God thus to honor the dear poor." As a result, a few of the sisters asked rather timidly if they might do the same. And in fact, two years later, March 25, 1642, Louise de Marillac and four of her companions bound themselves by vow to God and to the service of the poor, in the church of Saint-Nicolas-du-Chardonnet in Paris. The first step had been taken.

If Louise de Marillac and Vincent de Paul envisaged a vowed life for the Daughters of Charity, it was because they saw the commitment to and the contemplation of Jesus Christ as the root of all apostolic action. The vows were but a means to a more perfect imitation of the poor, chaste and obedient Christ who came upon earth to do good. United to Him, the sisters would dedicate their entire existence to the service of the poor, the sick and the unfortunate.

For Louise de Marillac, the vows represented the fullness of the grace of baptism. This awareness is explicit in the vow formula: "I renew the promises of my baptism . . ." They were also rooted in the Gospel. After the example of Jesus Christ, the Daughters of Charity bound themselves to live poorly, chastely and obediently. Freed from the desire for gain, the entanglements of the heart and the thirst for power, they could thus be more available to the poor to whose "corporal and spiritual service" they gave their lives.

This was the touchstone of the originality of the vocation of the Daughters of Charity as the founders conceived it. Poverty, chastity and obedience took their form and their meaning from the service of the poor. The vow formula, written in Louise's own hand, read: "In order to give myself, for this entire year, to the corporal and spiritual service of the poor, our true masters . . ." The expression "in order to" is significant, as is "for this entire year."

As surprising as it may appear, this concept of annual vows was clearly in keeping with the prudence and wisdom of Vincent de Paul and Louise de Marillac. (It was not a practice from the beginning; the earliest vows pronounced by the sisters were perpetual.) Reflection and experience prompted it, rather than any fear concerning the perseverance of the sisters. This was evident in the writings of the founders. On July 17, 1656, Louise wrote, "We do not accept girls who do not intend to live and die in the Company." Three years earlier, on June 3, 1653, Vincent had spoken to the sisters on the fidelity that they owed to God. He reminded them:

> Your first reason for giving yourself entirely to God so as to be faithful to Him, is that you have given yourselves to Him in the Company with the intention of living and dying in it. When you entered you promised to do so; some of you, indeed, have solemnly promised to do so.

In her correspondence, Louise de Marillac explained to the sisters that annual vows, rather than placing a limitation on their gift to God, were a means for stimulating them to yet greater love because of the freedom they supposed. On March 17, 1651, she wrote, "Do you not think that it must be very pleasing to God when, at the end of the year, with full freedom of choice, you make a new sacrifice?" On

June 9 of the same year, she told another sister, "At the end of a year you can once again give yourself freely to God."

The letter of March 17 clarified another aspect of the question: "We must be submissive to our superiors, who in this important matter judge it sufficient to make this offering for a year and then to renew it annually." The fundamental consideration is apparent: the fear that perpetual vows would lead to the cloister.

Elsewhere, Louise and the sisters were even more precise on this point. Sister Jeanne told the Bishop of Nantes, who questioned her:

> Your Excellency, the vows which we make are not religious. They are simple vows which can be made anywhere, even by persons living in the world.

On June 29, 1656, Louise said, "Our vows are no different from those made by devout men and women living in the world."

All of this clearly indicated the secular nature of the Company. Vincent de Paul explained the motivation behind it:

> It is not that you do not have great respect for religious, but if you were cloistered, we would have to bid farewell to the service of the poor.

The recurring theme of all their thoughts and actions appears again: *Jesus Christ is present in the poor.*

Chapter IX

THE COMPANY OF CHARITY

The dynamism and creativity of the charitable action of Vincent de Paul and Louise de Marillac were due to their unusual ability to combine daring initiatives with prudent means and a constancy that nothing could shake. Louise wrote:

> Our Lord asks of us more confidence than prudence. This very confidence will cause us to be prudent as situations require it, without our even realizing it. Experience has shown this on numerous occasions.

The majority of the first Daughters of Charity were illiterate. This does not mean that they were unintelligent, but they did need the guidance provided by rules for their diverse activities. Moreover, they lived in small groups, sometimes even alone, far from the cradle of their vocations. From Paris they had been sent to Cahors and Calais in the North, to several provinces throughout France and even as far as Poland. To help them in their difficult way of life, the founders established structures which were both diversified and flexible.

The term "structure" has become pejorative in recent years, but the necessity for some stable form of organization to insure continuity was apparent from the beginning. In this respect Louise de Marillac was to prove herself the worthy niece of Michel de Marillac, who had developed the Code Michau for France. She saw to it that contracts with the administrations which requested the services of the Daughters of Charity were drawn up in proper form.

However, for Louise, the spirit which animated the lives of the sisters was more important than the juridical aspects of the rules. Thus she always began by stressing the essential element in all their actions: to serve the poor is to serve Jesus Christ Himself.

In the Particular Rules for the Sisters Employed with Children, she wrote:

> They shall consider that their duty is to serve the Child Jesus in the person of each child whom they raise, realizing that by so doing they have the honor of doing what the Blessed Virgin did for her dear Son. Since Jesus Christ Himself assures them that any service rendered to the least of His is rendered to Him, they shall strive to raise these poor children with the care and respect they would give to the person of Our Lord Himself.

In the Particular Rules for the Sisters of the Parishes, we read:

> In serving the sick, they should have God alone in view . . . they shall treat them with respect and humility, remembering that all harshness and disdain, as well as the services and the honor they render them, are directed to Our Lord Himself.

The Particular Rules for the Sisters Employed in Schools revealed the flexibility which Louise desired:

> They shall regulate as far as possible the hours

of instruction, except for that given to poor little girls who have to earn their living. They shall give these children special preference, provide for their needs, and receive them when they come.

A similar recommendation can be found in the Particular Rules for the Sisters of the Villages:

They shall also have the care of instructing poor girls, not only those who attend their school, but also those of whatever age they may be and at whatsoever time they may come; and they shall receive them, if they are unable to wait, even when they come during meals. They shall take particular care to instruct those who have little opportunity to attend school, such as those who tend animals, receiving them at the times and places they may meet them—not only in the villages, but even walking through the countryside.

Thus Louise de Marillac inscribed flexibility into the framework of the Rules of the Daughters of Charity. She was equally firm in stressing the fundamental spirit of their vocation. This was perfectly expressed in the Rules for the Sisters of the Hospital of Angers:

The Daughters of Charity are going to Angers to honor Our Lord, the Father of the Poor, and His holy Mother, and to assist the sick poor corporally and spiritually.

The first thing that Our Lord asks of them is that they love Him above all things and perform all their actions for love of Him; the second is that they cherish one another as sisters bound together by the bond of His love and that they love the sick poor as their lords, since Our Lord is in them and they are in Him.

The same spirit of charity was to animate the entire Company in the diversity of its activities. In 1640, some seven years after the birth of the little community, the works of the sisters had spread across France. On July 19 of that year, Vincent de Paul spoke to them on the spirit of their vocation. He said:

> Reflect, my Daughters, on the greatness of God's design in your regard and the grace He bestows on you by even now enabling you to serve so many poor people in so many different places. To do this entails different sorts of regulations. The Daughters in Angers have theirs; one sort is needed for those who serve poor little children, another for those who serve the poor at the Hotel-Dieu, another for those who serve the poor in the parishes, another for those who serve the poor convicts, and still another for those who remain at home, which they should look upon and love as their family. And all these rules should be based on the Common Rules.

In the Common Rules, there was an article consecrated to the need for flexibility and mobility. It was to be found in the part on spiritual practices, and it dealt with the problem of finding a balance between the spiritual and the apostolic demands of their vocation. It read:

> Although they should make no scruple of sometimes changing the hour of these exercises, or even of omitting one of them when the urgent necessities of the poor require it, still they shall take care never to fail in them through negligence, indevotion, or too great an inclination for exterior things,

which is sometimes cloaked under the pretext of charity.

Vincent de Paul and Louise de Marillac engraved on the hearts of their daughters the principle that everything must be subordinated to the "urgent necessities of the poor." On November 17, 1658, Vincent told them:

> Charity is above all rules. Someone comes to your door when you are at prayer to ask a sister to go to see a poor sick person who needs her. What should she do? She will do well to go off and leave her prayer, or rather to continue it, because such is God's will . . . That is called leaving God for God.

If the founder sought to free the sisters from any taint of legalism, he was also careful to remind them of their obligations to God. In the same Conference he stated:

> If you should be called to visit a sick person, then you should leave your prayer aside; but you should seek another time for it, and never omit it. Daughters of Charity ought to love prayer as the body loves the soul . . . A sister who does not pray or who prays in a way that is not fitting will barely drag herself along. She wears the dress but she does not have the spirit of a Daughter of Charity. If you have seen some who have gone out from among you, that was the reason.

Were these diversified and flexible structures the work of Vincent de Paul or of Louise de Marillac? History would seem to indicate that they were the result of a combined effort. In a letter to Louise, Vincent said:

> I found all that you told me concerning the

charity to be excellent, and ask you to propose these things to the sisters in so far as you judge it appropriate—or anything additional which might come to mind. I will send you the completed Rule by Sunday.

A few days later he wrote:

I have drawn up something suitable for Montreuil. Take a look at it. If something should be added or deleted, please let me know.

Confident collaboration was the mark of their relationship. This union of minds was also apparent in the Conferences of Saint Vincent de Paul to his Daughters of Charity. These simple dialogues began shortly after Louise and the sisters came together in her home on the rue Saint-Victor. By means of them Vincent sought to develop in these village girls an understanding of their calling. On July 31, 1634, he told them:

Divine Providence has brought the twelve of you together here with the intention, it would seem, that you should honor His human life on earth . . . And what did He principally do? After submitting His will in obedience to Mary and Joseph, He continually worked for His neighbor, visiting and healing the sick and teaching them the things necessary for their salvation.

One hundred twenty of these Conferences, faithfully transcribed by Louise de Marillac or one of her sisters, have come down to successive generations of Daughters of Charity, who find in them a spirit and a doctrine which is none other than that of the Gospel. In these simple dialogues are to be found their way of life, their spirituality and their apostolic motivation. They are not a methodical, didactic presentation, but rather the response to the events and needs which marked the little Company at its origin. When writing to Vincent to ask him to give a Conference, Louise said:

> Would it not be well to assemble our sisters so that they could share their thoughts, encourage one another and recognize the faults they may have committed in the service of the poor, in their dealings with the Ladies and in the cordiality they owe to one another?

In all these exchanges, the poor occupy the central place. The founder never failed to mention them, since they represented the "raison d'etre" of the Daughters of Charity. However, the service of the poor was always linked to the love of God, of which, according to Louise de Marillac, it constituted an "essential element." In the Conference of July 31, 1634, Vincent told the sisters:

> My Daughters, remember that when you leave prayer or Holy Mass to serve the poor, you are losing nothing, because serving the poor is going to God and you should see God in them. So be very careful in attending to all their needs . . . do not get angry with them and never speak harshly to them. They have enough to put up with in their misfortune . . . Weep with them; God has made you their consolers.

This same theme would be repeated over and over again as Vincent de Paul and Louise de Marillac sought to help the sisters to grow in an understanding and appreciation of their vocation and of their consecration in the midst of the world, which was an unheard-of thing in the seventeenth century. On June 14, 1643, Vincent said:

> You should also reflect that your chief business,
> the one which God especially requires of you, is
> diligence in serving the poor who are your lords.
> Oh yes, Sisters, they are your masters. Hence you
> should treat them gently and kindly, reflecting that
> it is for that purpose that God brought you
> together, for that purpose He established your
> Company.

The founders also drew up Rules for the Company which
would be explained and discussed during community exchanges. In a letter from Vincent de Paul to Louise de
Marillac, we read:

> I am forwarding the Act of Establishment of the
> Daughters of Charity. It is divided into three parts:
> 1) the means which Divine Providence employed to
> establish them; 2) their way of life until now; 3)
> Rules for their confraternity or association.

To facilitate community exchanges on the Rule, the
sisters were given an outline before each Conference so that
they could reflect and pray on the principal points to be discussed and prepare their own remarks. Prior to the Conference of December 25, 1658, they were asked to reflect
before God on:

> 1) The motives for loving our vocation more and
> more; 2) whatever may cause this love to grow
> cold or may hinder us from loving our vocation; 3)
> the means we should employ to enable us to love it
> more and more.

On the day of the Conference, Louise de Marillac and

each of the sisters expressed their thoughts on the subject proposed; Vincent de Paul or one of his missionaries then synthesized them and added any necessary reflections. Careful notes were taken and later transcribed, thus providing a rich source of spiritual nourishment for successive generations of Daughters of Charity.

Most frequently, Louise de Marillac proposed the topic for the exchanges. For example, Vincent de Paul began the Conference of September 19, 1649 by telling the sisters, "Mademoiselle Le Gras thought it would be well if we reflected together on the love of God. We shall divide the subject into three parts." When one of these simple village girls had difficulty in expressing herself, Vincent came to her aid. When another made a particularly good remark, he encouraged her: "Oh, what a beautiful thought, my Daughter!"

There was nothing artificial or pedantic in these Conferences which, nevertheless, treated of the principal concerns of the early Company: its spirit, its goal, its preservation, its approbation, its place in the Church, its direction, its administration. Others dealt with the spiritual life of the sisters: how to love God well, how to be faithful to Him, how to imitate Jesus Christ, how to make a good Holy Communion, how to pray, why and how one should confide in Divine Providence. Still other exchanges concentrated on community life: union among themselves, cordial respect, reconciliation, difficulties. In all of them, the service of the poor was central. Some even treated of specific apostolates such as the care of the foundlings or the nursing of the sick. There are even examples of Gospel sharing. On November 25, 1658, Vincent and his daughters reflected together on The Wise and the Foolish Virgins. He began the discussion with his usual simplicity:

Imagine, Sisters, that there are forty or fifty of you. If half were saved and the other half were to be numbered with these wretched virgins—Ah, Saviour, each one would have reason to say: "O Lord, shall I be of this number?" Or again: "Shall I be so happy as to be in the same position as those virgins who were found pleasing in the eyes of their spouse?"

The discussion followed: "Sister, what do you think?" After receiving several responses, he turned to another sister: "Sister Vincent, pray tell me, who are those who may be said to be asleep?" He then asked the same question of others present. And so it went, with each one expressing her thoughts simply and humbly.

When the topic seemed particularly important to him, Vincent did not hesitate to ask some direct questions. In a Conference on mental prayer we find the following exchange:

> Sister Anne from Saint-Germain-de-l'Auxerrois, my Child, do you make mental prayer every morning?
>
> Yes, Father, for half an hour, and sometimes for three-quarters . . .
>
> And you, Sister Henriette, who are with the galley slaves, do you pray?
>
> Father, we cannot hear the clock, and so sometimes we are not exact about it . . .
>
> Is there anyone here from Saint-Sulpice? Sister, are you exact about prayer?
>
> We make it sometimes, but we cannot always do so, on account of the medicine we must take to the poor.

When sisters were leaving for a new establishment in the provinces, Louise de Marillac called the community together and asked Vincent to give them some advice. So it was when they went to Le Mans-Hennebont in 1650, to Nantes in 1653, to Sedan in 1654, to La Fere and Arras in 1656, to Ussel in 1658 and to Calais, Metz, Narbonne and Cahors in 1659.

On January 1, 1654, Vincent devoted an entire Conference to the topic, "How to Behave When Living Away From the Motherhouse." He began by asking, "Sister, does it behoove us to have a clear knowledge of how to behave when outside the house?" To this the sister responded:

> Yes, Father, for if we do not know how to behave, great disorders may arise; things might be said and done that would be quite contrary to the spirit of the Company. It might also happen that, through our fault, on account of our ignorance of our obligations, the poor might not be provided with all that they need.

Once again the poor were a major preoccupation. The same thing would be true when the sisters gathered to share their recollections of their companions who had died. On March 25, 1643, they assembled at the motherhouse to reflect on the virtues of Sister Jeanne Dalmagne, who had died thirty-three months earlier.

Vincent de Paul began the Conference:

> My dear Sisters, we have met, according to the holy custom of the Company, to speak of the virtues of our deceased sisters. O my Daughters, what a good thing it is to converse together on the good actions of the dead. The Holy Spirit desires us to do so.
>
> Hence, my dear Sisters, it will be a consolation for you to tell us what you have noticed in this dear sister ... Let us begin. You have all made your prayer as usual on the three points proposed. Tell us,

Sister, what you remarked in our good sister.

And so, each in turn, they shared their remembrances:

She had great respect for the poor in whom she saw God . . .

She had the utmost compassion for the poor. When unable to assist them corporally, she consoled them. She wept with them . . .

She always sought to bring relief to the poor . . . When I used to say to her, "Sister, you can give it to them," she used to say, "Oh no, Sister, I will eat that myself; we should not give God anything but the best . . ."

She had great liberty of spirit in everything that concerned the glory of God, and she spoke quite frankly to the rich as to the poor, whenever she saw anything blameworthy in their conduct. One day, when she learned that certain rich people had evaded their taxes and had managed to transfer them to the poor, she told them quite openly that such conduct was contrary to justice and that God would punish them for such extortions. And when I remarked to her that she had spoken out very bravely, she answered that when it was a question of God's glory and the welfare of the poor, one should never fear to speak the truth . . .

Even in her illness, she spoke of the poor with such fervor that it seemed that she shared in their suffering . . .

One evening, thinking that death was at hand, she said, "Sister, if I feel any regret it is for not having served the poor well. I beg you, serve them better. You are most happy to have been called by God to this vocation."

The great love for the poor which filled the heart of Louise de Marillac had been transmitted to the village girls whom she had formed for their service. Thus Vincent de Paul could conclude these exchanges by saying, "I have read many lives of saints. Few have surpassed our sister in the love of God and of the neighbor."

Jeanne was not the only one. This is clear from the response of Barbe Angiboust to the Duchess of Aiguillon, who wanted to keep her in her service to carry out her liberalities to the poor. Barbe told her:

> Madame, I left my father's home to serve the poor . . . if you were poor, I would willingly serve you.

She then left the duchess' household to return to the service of the poor.

The moment would come when the various apostolates which had sprung up in response to the urgent calls of the poor had to be coordinated. By 1641, in addition to serving the poor in the parishes and caring for the foundlings and the galley slaves, the sisters were nursing the sick in hospitals and teaching little girls in country areas. And that was but the beginning. New appeals were always being addressed to them.

Thus in 1646, after years of prayer and planning, Louise de Marillac and Vincent de Paul, confident of the support of the Queen, sought and obtained the approbation of the Archbishop of Paris for the little Company. Once assured of the recognition of the Church in France, the founders set about involving the sisters directly in the administration of the community. Revealing unusual supernatural and human wisdom, the founders assembled the sisters who were to make up the first Council of the Company on June 28, 1646. Vincent said to them:

By the grace of God, my Sisters, this Council which Divine Providence has established will be a step toward order and stability in your Company. We are assembled here to give our advice on certain necessary business as well as on the way in which you should govern yourselves, and to determine how Mademoiselle Le Gras or the Sister Servant [as the superior is called] should conduct the meetings.

Vincent then went on to point out the disposition which should characterize the deliberations: prayer to the Holy Spirit, openness to the inspirations of the Holy Spirit, detachment from any interest save the greater glory of God and the good of the Company, secrecy concerning all proceedings.

He then explained the manner in which they should proceed with the business before them:

It is incumbent on the Sister Servant, who at present is Mademoiselle Le Gras, to propose the matters to be discussed. Now in any question, there are always pros and cons. Thus in presenting the matter, she should first state the reasons for doing it, and then those which might prevent the Company from doing so. For example, she should say, "We should do such and such a thing for the following reasons. However, there are other considerations which we should bear in mind before acting."

Once this had been done, each sister in turn would be asked to give her opinion and the reasons supporting it. The final decision, however, would be that of the Superioress:

After the Sister Servant has heard all the opinions, she will follow the one she judges most appropriate. If she does not find any of them acceptable, she will say, "We will not settle this matter today. We will reflect on it before God." If she wishes to seek further advice, she may say, "I will discuss this with Father Vincent. We will see what will be best."

The minutes of twenty-nine of these Council meetings are extant. They treat of the principal concerns of the nascent community: the admission of new members, the transfer of sisters from one house to another, difficulties which had arisen and the means proposed for remedying them, and new foundations. The details of these discussions are unquestionably rooted in the life of the seventeenth century, but the problems and the proposed solutions are still current.

At the meeting of June 19, 1647, Vincent de Paul gave a directive of major importance to the first four sisters who had been chosen to participate in the government of the Company. He recognized their lack of experience, but stressed the need to use their native intelligence to discern the will of God. He told them:

God bestows His special blessing on this Council assembled to study matters which affect His service. This is why I tell you that, in order to learn how to deliberate on these questions which have been submitted to you, you must first of all examine the goal of all your actions: the glory of God. After that, you must consider the interests of the Company and the good of those whose lives will be affected by your decision.

We must first of all seek the glory of God and ask ourselves, "If we do this, will God be glorified? Will the community derive some advantage from it? Will our neighbor be assisted?"

He then gave an example:

> Let us suppose that we are considering sending Sister Jeanne to visit the sisters in Angers and Nantes to reflect with them on their dispositions with regard to their vocation.
>
> Before deciding anything at all, we must first determine whether or not God's interest would be served. There are many communities who consider the interest of the community first, believing that this is so great that it encompasses that of God. However, I feel that God merits to be thought of in the first place. Everything else, it would seem, is dependent on that.

The minutes of these Council meetings reveal the solid base on which the young Company was established. They contain norms for the apostolic life, tenets of prudence and wisdom for successive generations of Daughters of Charity.

Directly or indirectly, the poor were present in all of these deliberations. The Council met to decide if it was "expedient to send two sisters each afternoon to visit the sick poor of the parish, to console them." Elsewhere it was recorded:

> The first matter to be discussed is whether or not we should send sisters to Picardie to assist Sister Guillemine and three other sisters who had been sent there a long time ago to serve the sick and poor of this region which the war of the previous year had reduced to ruin.

So that the poor would be well served, they sought the means to have good servants of the poor and to collaborate with other persons and groups who were caring for them. On several occasions, Louise de Marillac and Vincent de Paul raised the question of the conditions for admission into the Company. Louise said that she particularly feared "flightiness which would make some young women totally unsuited for the service of the poor." Vincent would then elaborate on this point:

It is certainly true that one must be called by God to any vocation. Without such a call, there is nothing but wavering and inconstancy. A vocation from God is essential, if one is to persevere. This is why you must give yourselves to God so as to choose well among the persons who seek admission into the Company. You must ascertain, as far as possible, whether or not they have the physical, mental and spiritual qualities necessary for a Daughter of Charity. We must be very careful of this, otherwise we will turn the Company into an infirmary where other Daughters of Charity will be needed to care for the members rather than to serve the poor.

On yet another occasion, Vincent said to the members of the Council:

Religious congregations require large dowries of candidates seeking admission. You have only your poor and the Providence of God, which is already a great deal. It is in God and His care for you that you must place all your confidence.

Little by little, the young Company developed its structure and organization. At the Council meeting of April 13, 1651, Vincent de Paul pointed out the necessity of having sisters trained in administration. He said:

103

It is essential, my Daughters, to have sisters who will serve as councilors to the Superioress. However, we must all be persuaded of the necessity of changing the Sister Assistant and the other councilors from time to time. This should be done, firstly, to prevent them from becoming attached to this office. Secondly, it is advisable to have several sisters prepared to serve in this capacity. The good of the Company depends on the care of the councilors for the entire family.

On July 27, 1656, Vincent reminded Louise de Marillac and her councilors of the seriousness of their responsibilities. He told them:

Just as a compass continues to guide a ship which is tossed about by the wind, so superiors, although they are buffeted by conflicting opinions, must never cease to carry on the business of the Company in the way that God directs.

The founders did not seek mere approbation for decisions which had already been made. Rather, they sought the honest, personal opinion of each councilor.

When a new member of the Council protested that she was incapable of judging what should be done in a particular situation and urged Vincent to do what he believed best, he advised her to listen to the views of the others and then to give her own opinion. The minutes of the meeting of February 29, 1658 show that Louise de Marillac also placed a very high value on the advice which she received from her councilors. She expressed her fear that, through deference, the sisters might hide their true thoughts—to which Vincent responded:

O, my dear Daughters, you must never feel that

you must agree with the Superioress. Mademoiselle Le Gras wants you to know that it is her desire that you express yourselves freely in response to the inspirations which you have received from God, without being influenced by what you believe to be her point of view. Unless you act in this way, you are not a council assembled in God's name. It is to give advice that God has called you here to serve in the government of the community. Thus you are obliged to express your opinion with great simplicity despite the fact that, because of circumstances which cannot always be explained, there will be times when it will not be followed.

As the "little Company" grew, Vincent de Paul and Louise de Marillac formalized their vision of the exercise of authority in the community. Roles were clearly defined. The councilors were to give advice. The Superioress was to make the decisions. Together they were to seek to discern and to accomplish the will of God.

For both founders, authority was rooted in fraternal charity. This concept was beautifully expressed by Vincent at the Council meeting of June 19, 1647. They had come together to name two sisters for a new foundation. Louise suggested Sister Anne and Sister Marie Lullen, who had considerable experience in nursing the sick and caring for children. They were capable of functioning independently and well, but more importantly for the Superioress, they could help one another so that in time of need neither would say, "That is not my concern." Louise's remarks prompted Vincent to elaborate his trinitarian vision of authority:

For a long time I have hoped and prayed that our sisters would reach such a level of mutual respect that an outsider would never know which of them was the Sister Servant. My Daughters, God is one in Himself, but in God there are three Divine Persons. Yet the Father is not greater than the Son nor is the Son greater than the Holy Spirit. The Company of the Daughters of Charity must be an image of the Trinity. Although they are many, they must have but one heart and one spirit.

Different operations are attributed to each Person of the Blessed Trinity, yet they are all interrelated. The wisdom of the Son, the goodness of the Holy Spirit in no way diminish the power of the Father. The Holy Spirit shares in the attributes of the Father and of the Son. So, Daughters of Charity who serve the poor share in the apostolic work of those who care for children. And those who care for children participate in the service of the poor.

My desire is to see our sisters resemble the Blessed Trinity. Just as the Holy Spirit proceeds from the total union of the Father and the Son, so the works of charity attributed to the Spirit will result from a union of minds and hearts in the community.

You see, my Daughters, God is Charity. You are Daughters of Charity. You must, therefore, do all in your power to be formed in the image of God. And what do we find in God? We see equality of persons and unity of essence. What should that teach you if not that you should all be one and equal?

Maintaining this unity would become more difficult with the passage of time. As the sisters became more numerous, they set out, often in groups of two or three, to establish foundations throughout France and beyond. Travel was difficult, sometimes dangerous. It took ten to fifteen days to reach some houses. A trip to Poland required six months.

So it was that Louise de Marillac sought to strengthen the bonds of unity by means of a prolific correspondence. There are still extant 650 letters, dating from 1627 to 1660.

Louise de Marillac knew, from personal experience, the supportive value of correspondence. As a young wife and widow she had needed help. It was at that period that she began writing to Vincent de Paul. In the beginning they wrote frequently. As the years passed and she grew more independent, both spiritually and psychologically, they corresponded less. After 1641, when the motherhouse of the Daughters of Charity was established very close to the Priory of Saint-Lazare, personal contact replaced correspondence, for the most part. Nevertheless, there are more than 200 letters spanning a period of thirty-three years.

With the foundation of the Hospital of Angers in 1639, Louise began what would prove to be a very lengthy correspondence with Father Guy Lasnier, known also as the Abbe de Vaux. This outstanding priest had experienced a spiritual conversion during a retreat at Saint-Lazare preached by Vincent de Paul, whose acquaintance he made. Following his conversion, he devoted himself entirely to the spiritual reorganization of the Hospital of Saint-Jean at Angers. In this work, he was aided by Madame Goussault, a Lady of Charity whom Vincent de Paul greatly admired. Through her he was able to obtain the services of eight Daughters of Charity to nurse the sick. Louise de Marillac went to Angers to organize the work. Her interest and concern never diminished, as is evidenced by her frequent letters to Father Lasnier and to the first sisters assigned there. The Hospital of Saint-Jean was to be the prototype for all subsequent institutional health care. Louise herself composed the Rule of Life for the sisters there. A copy in Vincent's handwriting is still extant. It reflects the spirituality of the young Company: *to honor Our Lord Jesus Christ as the source and model of all charity.* It also stresses the role of the Daughter of Charity as *servant of the poor.* It reads:

> The Daughters of Charity shall recall that they
> were born poor and must live poorly for the love of
> Jesus Christ Our Lord, the Father of the Poor.
> Thus they must be humble and respectful with
> everyone . . . dress poorly . . . and manage the
> goods of the poor as the property of God.

Father Lasnier served as spiritual director for the sisters
in this first mission established far from Paris. However, the
more than 100 letters of Louise to him and to the sisters, as
well as her frequent reminder of the article of the Rule of
Life which stated, "They shall write frequently to their
Superiors in Paris . . ." show that she remained united to
them in heart and spirit.

Soon Angers would no longer be the only distant mission.
The nearly sixty letters addressed to Sister Barbe Angiboust
reveal the mobility and flexibility of the early community,
as this indefatigable Daughter of Charity was to be found at
the service of the poor in Richelieu, Liancourt, Bicetre,
Saint-Denis, Brienne, Chalons, Bernay and Chateaudun.

The letters to Sister Barbe Angiboust show the concern
of the Superioress for the service of the poor. However, her
correspondence was never limited to apostolic considerations. As nothing else does, the letters of Louise de Marillac
to her companions reveal her warmth, her affection for
them and her deep, personal interest in everything that
touched their lives. Those who were experiencing personal,
community, or apostolic difficulties received particular
signs of her solicitude in the form of letters of support and
encouragement. There are some fifty letters addressed to
Sister Jeanne Lepintre, who struggled against enormous
obstacles at the Hospital of Nantes, from which the sisters
were eventually obliged to withdraw. Another thirty went to
Sister Julienne Loret, the Sister Servant of the House of

Charity at Chars, where a Jansenist pastor was publicly refusing to permit the sisters to receive Holy Communion. In good times and bad, the Superioress was close to her sisters wherever they served the poor.

Besides revealing the personality of the woman who had founded the "little Company," the correspondence of Louise de Marillac provides insight into the nature of the community. Its secular nature, something totally unheard-of at the time, is clarified in a letter to Vincent de Paul dated April, 1650. She wrote:

> Yesterday I went to see the Procurator General . . . He asked me if we intended to be regular or secular. I told him secular. He said that this was unprecedented . . . but that he did not disapprove of the idea. He spoke highly of the Company; however, he thought that a matter of such importance should be carefully considered.
>
> I expressed my joy that he felt as he did, and begged him to destroy the Company completely if it did not deserve to continue. However, if he considered it good, I urged him to establish it on a solid base. I explained that we had given it a trial period of nearly fifteen years to determine its viability, and that, by the grace of God, we had encountered no insurmountable obstacles. He asked for time to reflect on the matter . . . and sent you his best regards.

This concern of Louise de Marillac to safeguard the secular nature of the community is affirmed in a letter of June 29, 1656, to Father Lasnier. She sought to avoid any confusion which might arise concerning the vows pronounced by the Daughters of Charity. She told him:

> I am afraid that Sister Jeanne Lepintre has de-

scribed the vows in such a way that others may consider them the same as those pronounced by devout lay persons. Such is not the case, since these persons usually pronounce them before their confessor.

This concern led Louise to present the matter to Vincent de Paul. In response to her question as to whether or not the sisters should be allowed to make vows privately he said:

> We should be very careful in this matter. However, should there be individual sisters who wish to do so, they may present their request to superiors and then abide by their decision.

This text clearly shows that, for the founders, the Company was secular but it was not lay. They were careful to distinguish between a personal, individual consecration to God made by the laity, and the consecration of the Daughter of Charity which was made with others within what they both referred to as "a body within the Church." Vincent de Paul returned to this question in the Conference of September 22, 1647 on Perseverance in Our Vocation. He told the assembled community:

> It would be well if those on whom God has bestowed the grace of giving themselves more perfectly to Him and who have promised to serve Him in the Company were to renew their vows. Oh yes, that would be well. That gives new strength and draws down new graces. Those who can do so and who are in this state should adopt this means with humility and with the confidence that God will assist them; those who are not yet bound by vows should renew their resolutions.

Elsewhere Vincent stressed the seriousness of the commitment made by vows in the Company when he told the sisters, "It would be better not to make them than to be ready to dispense oneself from them whenever one so desired."

The commitment of the Daughters of Charity was to God and to the Company. Louise de Marillac explained this situation, which was unique in the Church at the time, in a letter to Father Lasnier. She wrote:

> Please let me know, Father, if there is anything in the first article of the Rule of Life of our sisters which would mark us as a religious congregation . . . This has never been my intention. On the contrary, I have been to the Vicar General two or three times to explain to him that we are a secular family bound together by the Confraternities of Charity. Vincent de Paul, who is Superior of these Confraternities, is our director.

This bond with the Superior General of the Congregation of the Mission marked the Company of the Daughters of Charity from its inception. In the mind of Louise de Marillac it was essential to preserve the unity of the community and its goal: *the service of Christ in the poor.* On July 5, 1651, she wrote to Vincent de Paul:

> The Company must be established with the title of Company or Confraternity so that it may continue to exist and give God the glory it appears capable of rendering Him. Moreover, it must be entirely submissive to and dependent on the venerable guidance of the Most Honored Father General and the venerable Priests of the Mission.

Five years earlier, Louise had expressed her concern that

the term "dependence on the Archbishop of Paris," which appeared in the Act of Approbation of the Company in 1645, "might be harmful to us in the future by the freedom it implies to withdraw us from the direction of the Superior General of the Mission." She urged Vincent to rectify the situation:

> In the name of God, my Father, do not let any-thing even remotely withdraw the Company from the direction God has given to it. You may be cer-tain that very quickly it would change from what it now is. The sick poor would no longer be cared for, and thus, I believe, the will of God would cease to be accomplished among us.

The perseverance of Louise de Marillac would finally overcome all obstacles. The Company was approved by the Archbishop of Paris once again in 1655. This time the direction was confided exclusively to the Superior General of the Congregation of the Mission and his delegates. The unity of spirit and the continued service of the poor were safeguarded.

It is in the correspondence of Louise de Marillac that the roots of the devotion of the community to the Mother of God are to be found. On December 8, 1658, she wrote to Vincent de Paul requesting that the Virgin Mary be desig-nated the "Mother of the Company." In October 1644, she had made a pilgrimage to Chartres to place the entire com-munity under the protection of Mary. In her account we read:

> I offered to God the designs of His Providence on the Company of the Daughters of Charity. I dedicated it entirely to Him, declaring that I would rather see it destroyed than established against His holy will. I asked Our Lady, the Mother and

guardian of the Company, for the purity . . . fidelity . . . and union of hearts it requires.

Two hundred years later, as if to show her acceptance of her role and of the foundress' gift, Mary confided the Medal of the Immaculate Conception, known popularly as the "Miraculous Medal," to a Daughter of Charity, Saint Catherine Labouré. In 1830 Mary told her young confidant:

> Come to the foot of the altar. Here graces will be bestowed upon all who ask for them with confidence and fervor. They will be granted to great and small alike.

Mary, as it were, ratified the principal goal of the Company founded by Louise de Marillac and Vincent de Paul: the service of the poor, of the "small ones" of this world. Indeed, it was in 1830, following Mary's promise that "God would make use of it to reanimate the Faith," that the community began its expansion into the five continents of the earth. The words of the founder to the Priests of the Mission could now be applied to his daughters:

> Our vocation is not to a parish or a diocese but to the entire world. And what are we called to do? To enflame the hearts of men, to do what the Son of God did. And what did He do? He came to spread fire upon the earth so that it might be enflamed with His love. What are we to desire but that it burn and consume all?

The vocation of the Daughters of Charity, with the total gift of self which it demanded, is defined in practical terms by Louise de Marillac in a letter addressed to Brother Ducournau, Vincent's secretary, in January of 1658. It concerns some young women who were seeking admission into the Company. She told him:

> These girls . . . who want to join the Daughters of Charity must be informed that we are not a religious order. Neither can they work in one hospital and never be moved. They must continually go in search of the sick poor in different places and give them efficient service. They must know that they will be very poorly clothed and nourished and that . . . when they join the Company they must have no other desire than to serve God and their neighbor with their whole being.

For Louise de Marillac as for Catherine of Siena, the love of God and the love of neighbor were inseparable. The foundress frequently quoted God's words to this ardent soul to her first Daughters of Charity:

> A soul who truly loves Me also loves his neighbor, since love for Me and love of the neighbor are one and the same. Your love for your neighbor is the measure of your love for Me. I have given you this means for proving and exercising your love for Me. You are useful to Me to the extent that you are useful to your neighbor. The soul who loves My truth never wearies of devoting himself to the service of others.

Two hundred years later, another saint, John of the Cross, would say much the same thing:

> As the love of neighbor grows, the love of God increases in us. Likewise the more we love God, the greater will be our love of the neighbor since both of these loves have the same object and the

same cause.

Louise de Marillac translated this Gospel counsel by calling the neighbor the "representative of God." Her ever-increasing love of the poor, which gave meaning and direction to her life and which she transmitted to her daughters, was rooted in this conviction. She constantly reminded them:

> If we forget for a moment that the poor are the members of Jesus Christ, we will inevitably serve them with less gentleness and love ... We must therefore be persuaded that the poor are the members of the Son of God.

The service of Jesus Christ in the person of the poor was the unifying force in the lives of the Daughters of Charity. All their time and energy was to be expended for the love and service of God and their neighbor. On May 4, 1650, Louise wrote to Sister Cecile Agnes:

> In the name of God, my Sister, I urge you to be very gentle and courteous to the poor. You know they are our masters and that we must love them tenderly and respect them greatly. It is not enough for these sentiments to be deeply rooted in our hearts. We must bear witness to them by gentle, loving care.

The vocation of the Daughters of Charity called them to share the lot of the poor. The early community grew in the midst of wars, epidemics, floods and famine. Louise de Marillac worried about the well-being of her sisters, but she never failed, when offering her support and comfort, to remind them of the plight of the poor to whose service they had vowed their lives. To the sisters at the Hospital in

Angers, she wrote:

> The account of the misfortunes which have befallen Angers has made me keenly aware of the sufferings of the poor. I beg the Divine Goodness to console them and to afford them the help that they need . . . You, my Sisters, have also suffered greatly. Have you reflected that it is just that the servants should suffer with their masters?

On June 11, 1652, Louise wrote to the sisters in Brienne, who were likewise sharing in the hardships of the poor. She exhorted them:

> Bear their sufferings with them. Provide what assistance you can and remain at peace. Are you yourselves in need? You should be consoled. If you had an abundance, you would feel guilty in using it while witnessing the privations of our lords and masters.

The motivation for this total gift of self to the service of the poor was always "the pure love of God." Frequently, the response to charity was not only ingratitude but open aggression. On one such occasion, Louise wrote:

> O, my Sisters, if you knew how consoled I was recently when I heard that one of our sisters had been struck by a poor person and had done nothing to defend herself. Alas, he was a hard master, but we must put up with his attack. We are the servants of the poor and must endure their abuse.

Louise urged the sisters to spiritualize their personal suffering by uniting it to that of Christ, and never to forget the needs of the poor. When Sister Barbe was ill, she encouraged her "not to become weary of finding herself in a situation in which she, like her masters the poor, has need of help, cordiality and gentleness." She saw personal suffering as a means for growing in compassion. When a sister had recovered from a particularly painful illness, she wrote, "Oh, what compassionate love she will have for the sick poor after such long suffering!"

The sister infirmarian was encouraged to direct the thoughts of her sick companions toward the plight of the sick poor whom they were all called to serve:

> On your bed of pain, reflect on the sufferings of our poor sick who are often alone, without a fire. They often sleep on straw with neither sheets nor blankets to make them comfortable. They experience little gentleness or consolation.

However, it was not only at times of suffering or need that the sisters were called upon to share the life of the poor. As servants, they were also bound by the law of work. Louise reminded them, "All your time is given to the service of the poor." Elsewhere she said, "If you have any free time, use it to earn money for the poor or in instructing them in the things necessary for their salvation." She frequently asked them, "Is there any work available for you in the city? Do not forget that it is our practice to earn our own livelihood." But even here, the service of the poor was the motivating force. Louise told her companions, "You must work not only to support yourselves—as your masters, the poor, do—but also to provide for them."

Louise de Marillac saw the law of work as applying not only to the individual sister, but also to the community as a whole. She wrote:

> Oh, what a happiness it would be if, without offending God, the Company could devote itself to

the service of the most destitute . . . if Divine Providence could furnish it with more than minimum
necessities, thus permitting the sisters to go, at their
own expense, to provide for the corporal and
spiritual needs of the very poorest. It would not
matter if the work passed unnoticed, so long as
souls continued to honor the merits of the Redemp-
tion of Our Lord Jesus Christ for all eternity.

These words make it clear that the service of the poor
was not philanthropy, but the total gift of self. Louise
placed before her daughters the example of Jesus Christ:

Imitate, as far as you can, Our Lord, who poured
out His strength and His very life in the
service of others.

The management of the goods of the poor required strict
justice and scrupulous honesty, because, according to
Louise, "The property of the poor is the property of God
Himself." She reminded Sister Julienne Loret, at the House
of Charity in Chars, to "be careful never to use anything
belonging to the poor." She even went beyond justice to ask
for sacrifices, big and small, to provide better service to the
poor. When a sister sent her some fruit, she thanked her,
but then added:

I am delighted with your excellent fruit, but
please do not deprive your poor. Always satisfy
their needs with the best you have. It is their due.

As servants of the poor, the Daughters of Charity were
called upon to live like the poor in sickness and in health. In
the Common Rules we read:

They shall content themselves with the common

treatment of the poor with regard to medicine, food and other similar necessities . . . They shall consider, particularly in this case, that the servants of the poor ought not to be better attended than their masters . . .

However, Vincent de Paul and Louise de Marillac recognized that even this sharing of the life of the poor was not sufficient to insure effective service. The sisters were called upon to collaborate with all sorts of people. This required yet another form of abnegation. Louise urged them:

> For the love of God, my Sisters, be gentle with the poor and with all those with whom you come in contact. Try to be accommodating in words and actions. This will be easy enough if you maintain great respect for your neighbor.
>
> Oh, how I pray that you will be loved. This is so necessary in the places to which Divine Providence has called you. At all times let it be seen that you seek only the good of the poor whom you serve.

It would appear that, despite human failures, they were able to bring the love of God to those in need by their total gift of themselves to the service of Christ in the person of the poor. Vincent de Paul reinforced this belief in his Conference of March 4, 1658, when he said:

> My Daughters, the name of each of you was written in the book of charity when you gave yourselves to God to serve the poor, and in particular, on the day on which you made your vows you received this name which God has given to you. Therefore, you should live in conformity with the name you bear, since it was God Himself who gave it to the Company . . . it was the people who, seeing

what you were doing and the service which our first sisters rendered to the poor, gave you this name, which has remained as one most suitable to your way of life.

In a period of some thirty years, Vincent de Paul and Louise de Marillac had succeeded in transmitting their love for the poor to these simple village girls, who, like them, would give their all for the service of "the members of Jesus Christ." One of them spoke the sentiments of all during the Conference of December 8, 1659, a few short months before the death of Louise de Marillac and of Vincent de Paul, when she exclaimed:

Oh, if I had the strength I would want to serve the poor for the rest of my life and even until the end of time, that God might be glorified!

At the beginning of 1660, old age was taking its toll. Both Vincent and Louise felt the constraints imposed upon them by failing health. Shortly before her death on March 15, 1660, Louise wrote:

It takes great courage to accept the incapacity to act when it pleases God to ask this of us, and to use this suffering to rise above the things of earth. However, this should cause us to reflect that God desires that, after having worked all our lives for our neighbor, we should take time to prepare for Heaven, which is our blessed homeland.

Several years earlier, in a letter dated December 13, 1647, Vincent de Paul had sketched a portrait of this frail, dynamic woman. He wrote:

I consider Mademoiselle Le Gras as having been

all but dead for the past ten years. Looking at her, one would think that she had come forth from the grave, her face is so pale. But only God knows her strength of spirit. Not long ago she went on a very long trip, and only frequent bouts of illness and her respect for obedience prevented her from going yet farther to visit her daughters and to work with them, although only the grace of God kept her alive.

Until her last breath, her thoughts and her prayers were with her sisters and with the poor. She wanted to be kept informed of the care given to the numerous poor who came to the motherhouse for food. She died as she had lived: a *Servant of the Poor.* Her last words to her daughters testify to her life and to her legacy:

Take great care to serve the poor;

Above all, live together in great union and cordiality;

Loving one another in imitation of the union and life of Our Lord;

Take the Blessed Virgin as your only mother.

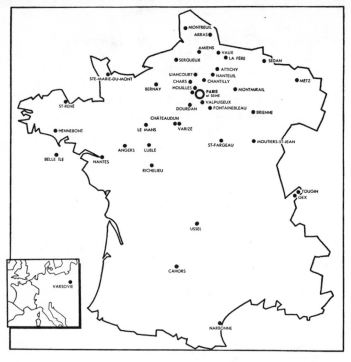

Houses of the Company in 1660, including 25 houses in Paris.

SOURCES

The original quotations of Louise de Marillac and Vincent de Paul found in this work are taken from the following:

Sainte Louise de Marillac: Correspondence 1627 - 1660, Meditations, pensees, avis. This work was published in 1961 from texts of manuscripts preserved in the archives of the motherhouse of the Daughters of Charity, 140 rue du Bac, Paris, France.

Saint Vincent de Paul: correspondence, entretiens, documents. 14 volumes. Edited by Pierre Coste. Paris: Lecoffre—Gabalda, 1925.

In addition to these two references, quotations were also taken from:

Baunard, Msgr. *Louise de Marillac (Mademoiselle Le Gras), fondatrice des Filles de la Charite de Saint Vincent de Paul.* Third Edition. Paris: Jean de Gigord, 1921. Of particular importance is the list of documents concerning the Daughters of Charity and Louise de Marillac preserved in the National Archives of France, found on page VII of this work.

Flinton, S. Margaret. *Sainte Louise de Marillac: l'aspect social de son oeuvre.* Brussels: Desclee, 1953.

124

Above: An early Conference. At these Conferences, St. Vincent instructed the Daughters, and with St. Louise they shared their thoughts on the vocation of a Daughter of Charity.

Opposite upper: St. Vincent and St. Louise discuss the needs of the poor.

Opposite lower: St. Vincent reads the Rule to the first Ladies of Charity. *(Drawings used with the kind permission of CEME Publishers, Salamanca, Spain.)*

125

St. Vincent, St. Louise (at St. Vincent's right), and Ladies of
Charity. In the foreground are foundlings, a Daughter of Charity,
and a wet nurse.

St. Vincent pleads with the Ladies of Charity not to abandon the foundlings: "If you abandon these little ones, what will God say, since it is He who has called you to care for them." St. Louise is the second from the right.

Daughters of Charity in the Hospital of Angers. St. Vincent urged them to care for the sick with great gentleness, seeing Jesus Christ in them.

An early Daughter of Charity carrying a drink to the sick.

St. Vincent and St. Louise in the Hospice of the Holy Name of Jesus, where the aged were cared for and enabled to continue working at their crafts. St. Vincent often came to speak to them about God.

Opposite: A close-up showing St. Louise.

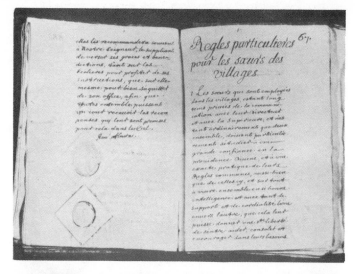

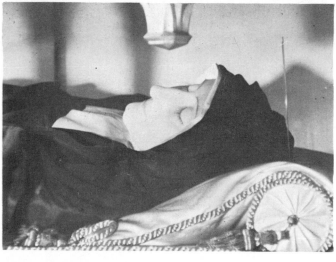

Upper: A page from The Particular Rules for the Sisters of the Villages.
Lower: Wax figure covering the relics of St. Louise in the chapel of the motherhouse.

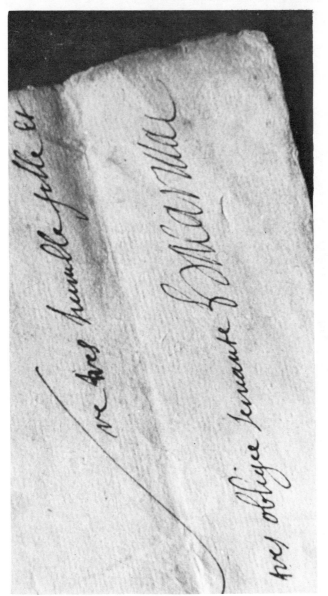

The signature of St. Louise de Marillac.

The seal of Louise de Marillac and the Company of the Daughters of Charity. The Latin inscription says *The Charity of Christ Impels Us.*

Stained glass window showing St. Louise, St. Vincent, and Daughters of Charity.

Statue of St. Louise de Marillac erected in St. Peter's Basilica, Rome, at the time of her canonization.